RESIDENTIAL SOCIAL WORK
General Editor: Tom Douglas

Interpreting Residential Life

Interpreting Residential Life
VALUES TO PRACTISE

James S. Atherton

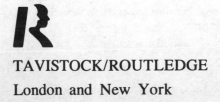

TAVISTOCK/ROUTLEDGE

London and New York

First published 1989 by Routledge
11 New Fetter Lane, London EC4P 4EE
29 West 35th Street, New York, NY 10001

© 1989 James S. Atherton
General Editor's Foreword © 1989 Tom Douglas
Photoset by Mayhew Typesetting, Bristol, England
Printed in Great Britain by Richard Clay Ltd, Bungay, Suffolk

British Library Cataloguing in Publication Data

Atherton, James S.
  Interpreting residential life: values to
  practise
  1. Residential care
  I. Title
  351'.05

  ISBN 0−415−00814−x
  ISBN 0−415−00815−8 Pbk

Library of Congress Cataloging-in-Publication Data

Atherton, James S., 1944−
  Interpreting residential life: values to practise / James S.
  Atherton
     p. cm. − (Residential social work)
  Bibliography: p.
  Includes index.
     1. Institutional care − Great Britain. 2. Social service − Great
Britain.   I. Title.   II. Series.
HV59.A84   1989
362'.0425−dc19   88−26801
                                                             CIP

ISBN 0−415−00814−X. − ISBN 0−415−00815−8 (pbk.)

Contents

To Susi,
from whom I have learned so much

Acknowledgements

A book such as this has two sources, both equally necessary – the ideas that become the theoretical framework, and the experiences and the background information about residential practice. Much of the latter has come from listening to hundreds of residential workers describe their practice and their problems, on courses and in their establishments; to list all of them would take at least another volume this size. I should particularly like to thank students in the Certificate in the Residential Care of Children and Young People courses at Salford College of Technology, and those on In-Service and short courses at Bedford College of Higher Education, who have unwittingly contributed to much to this book and sometimes had to sit through it in the form of lectures. My colleagues at both colleges have stimulated me with discussions about both theory and practice, as have all my fellow members of the Independent Review of Residential Care (the Wagner Committee). It is always invidious to select any individuals from such groupings, but I have gained so much from discussions with Des Kelly, Phylidda Parsloe, Chris Payne, Malcolm Payne, Patrick Phelan, and Martin Weinberg, and the chairing of Gillian Wagner, that I must mention them. The Committee was the best kind of advanced seminar on residential work imaginable, and led to the refinement of many of the ideas expressed here. Without the support of my colleagues in Bedford it would not have been possible to enjoy the privilege of participation in such a group.

The test of residential practice is in the experience of its consumers, and I must thank sincerely all those who have shared their perspective, either on all too brief acquaintance in many establishments, or through written contributions to the Wagner Committee, or through a closer relationship – especially George, Robert, Keith, and Donna.

It is always valuable to discuss with practitioners how they have gone about translating their visions and convictions into practice, and among many I must mention first Susi, my wife, who will certainly be impatient with some of the theorizing contained in this book, but whose experience and reflection are essential elements of it. Barbara Aldwinckle, Arnold Critchley, and Wilf Godman have also helped to develop the thinking through discussions of their own excellent practice. Participants in the series of conferences organized by the Planned Environment Therapy Trust and the Association of Therapeutic Communities have given great insight into therapeutic environments, and thanks are due to the planning committee members both for making these possible and for their personal contributions: Cynthia Cross, John Cross, Graeme Farquharson, Alan Fox, and Stuart Whiteley.

On the primarily theoretical side, I must thank my former colleagues at the Grubb Institute of Behavioural Studies, particularly Bruce Reed, Barry Palmer, Jean Hutton, John Bazalgette, and Colin Quine. Much of the systems-based side of the theory originally owes a lot to them, although they may well not wish to be identified with the final results!

As to the writing, Susi again deserves thanks for her contribution to the leg-work of research, and her toleration of my peculiar hours while writing. David Pithers and Peter Righton saw some of this material in advance (some of it long ago) and were both critical and encouraging. Tom Douglas read the manuscript and rightly insisted on an additional chapter.

All these people, and many others, must share in any credit for what follows. I assume full responsibility for its failings.

James S. Atherton
Bedford
April 1988

General Editor's Foreword

Providing the tools to help make sense of the apparent complexities of residential establishments is manifestly the fundamental aim of this series. But the problem has always been to define instruments that were neither so theoretical nor so essentially work-a-day as to suffer instant rejection by those to whom they were presented. James Atherton, by carefully selecting what he knows from personal experience to be an acceptable and comprehensible explanatory construction (i.e. systems theory), and by choosing some very important aspects of residential life, has used the former to elucidate the latter with a humour and clarity of expression that are seldom found in this area.

It is no longer good enough that the staff in residential establishments should be content, if indeed they ever were, to accept that they are powerless. One of Atherton's main themes is that such is the power of residential establishments over their residents, that it behoves all such workers at least to have some logical understanding of the possible consequences of that power, and that a selective use of it should be based on a consciously understood value system. It is essential in this context to define most clearly the difference between the probable lack of influence residential staff may have on the larger system (the organization of which their unit is but a part) and an all-encompassing influence and the way it is used, to which they have access in their own unit system.

I applaud this attempt by Atherton to lay down simple and direct guidelines for workers in residential systems to use to think about what they are trying to do. 'Caring' is a wholly inadequate omnibus word and in my experience is often used by people who are aware that its emotive connotations and widely accepted nature are a sufficient screen for a lack of real understanding of what it is they are actually doing.

Atherton in his teaching career has developed a method of relating complex ideas of proven value to simple key words or phrases. Two in this text are especially memorable – 'the working myth' and the 'skeleton/shell' concepts. They are so simple as to invite scorn, but yet with a little thought they are capable of the development of a truly practical understanding of apparently unrelated and different organizational practices.

The yawning gulf between the exciting explanatory idea and its development and use in practical methods of working has been and always will be a daunting and formidable obstacle to the growth of enhanced practice skill. The first step in this process is to provide appropriate explanatory ideas; the second is to take these ideas into the workplace and attempt to relate them to explicit areas of practice to be found there; the third is to use the general light of the ideas to illuminate particular situations and to modify the working practice accordingly.

This method of reviewing what is being done against acceptable ideas this becomes an input into the feedback loop aptly described here. Any system of whatever nature can only be as effective as the use it makes of the feedback that it receives. Atherton illustrates the applicability of this aphorism to the residential establishment.

Systems can and do engulf people, and what was set up as an effective means of meeting perceived needs often can and does become a self-perpetuating structure in which the greater part of the available energy is directed to maintaining the system in existence.

I hope that the great clarity with which this book is written will encourage workers in the residential field to review their work and to realize the great potential that exists but which is so often frustrated in its expression by a lack of the necessary understanding.

TOM DOUGLAS

Introduction

It is important to go back to first principles in a discussion of residential work because of the sheer *power* that residential workers (particularly Heads of Homes) wield over those for whom they 'care'. Very often they do not feel powerful, with the bureaucracy breathing down their necks all the time, but the staff are largely responsible for the quality of a substantial part of the lives of those who live in their establishments. Each of us has only one life. Residents have only one life each. It is enormously precious. What residential staff do (and do not do) every second of every day dictates in large measure the extent to which each resident can live his or her only life to the full. Any book about doing that must be a work of philosophy. But, in the words of William Blake:

> He who would do good to another must do it in Minute Particulars.
> General Good is the plea of the scoundrel, hypocrite and flatterer;
> For Art and Science cannot exist but in minutely organized Particulars.

So the philosophy has to be applied to severely practical matters. In this book therefore, we shall not be concerned with 'big' issues, but with the implications of those aspects of day-to-day care that also make a real difference to the quality of life of the residents – bathing, toileting, mealtimes, risk-taking, outings, and so on.

THE CENTRALITY OF VALUES

In the first sentence I put 'care' in quotes. The reason was not that I wish in any way to devalue the work undertaken by residential workers; but that while 'care' is a necessary shorthand word, it begs many questions – in particular about the needs of the users of services – and so it is used sparingly here, with no particular assumptions about the dependence of users. In this respect, I am trying to avoid the usual value judgement which presupposes that 'care' is a 'good thing'. On the other hand, I have also made a declaration about the preciousness of individual life. That is already a value judgement, and there are some cultures where it would not be shared, and if this book has one message, it is about the centrality of values to residential practice. There is, I believe, *absolutely nothing in residential practice that does not involve value questions*. Whether one is looking at waking people up in the mornings, giving them baths (or telling/persuading/asking/permitting them to have baths), resolving disputes, talking to relatives, ordering food, cleaning corridors, filling in returns, or chatting to colleagues over coffee, every bit of the day and night is filled with value judgements. Not only that, but there is no single set of values that fits every circumstance in residential work; so the reader will not find in this book any 'code of practice' or easy answers – just some more or less difficult questions.

The centrality of values stems from the power of residential workers mentioned above. Whether or not residential workers choose to exercise that power is itself a matter of value judgements.

Tutt (1973) pointed out that running a residential establishment is very similar to running a country, and that if one looks at most establishments on that basis, they are pretty totalitarian. What country would have a dominant elite group whose word is law and whom the majority of the population can never hope to join (the staff), routinely impose a curfew (specify bedtimes), keep secret files on inhabitants (residents), attempt to regulate or even forbid all sexual expression, impose punishments without trial, and so on? Only a dictatorship. And yet all these things and many more are routine in the majority of residential establishments. I can hear the reader muttering, 'But it's different in residential care!' Perhaps it is – but why, and how? Every social institution engages in the infringement of the rights of the individual, but that does not mean that it is not obliged to take seriously what it is up to.

The problem stems from the sheer pervasiveness of the residential task, its penetration into the most intimate areas of the residents' lives. If one includes nursing and penal provisions in residential work there is no other occupation (with the possible exception of parenting, which is in itself an informal variety of residential work) which routinely has so much effect on the continuing experience of its consumers. But workers in the field would be totally paralysed if they were to think too deeply about the minute-to-minute practice of their work. The nature of the task is that it demands practical activity at a moment's notice. There is very little time to think. Most of the situations confronting residential workers are repetitious if not entirely routine. Moreover, there is a need for consistency (that is a value judgement) between different staff members in handling situations, and the net result is that they come to rely on procedures, rules-of-thumb, and 'recipes' that are very concrete. They serve their purposes by treating all the value questions as solved for all practical purposes.

Since the problems are potentially overwhelming, many residential staff are not keen to raise them again. Even on training courses, there is a reluctance to look at them. They therefore rarely attract the attention of the kind of people who write books, and those books that *have* been written are rarely from the practitioner's point of view. Although the literature on residential work is growing, much of it is about the very important questions of when residential provision is indicated, and the form it ought to take in relation to wider society. Although it is possible to point to a stream of articles and books on the residential task (Payne, Douglas, and Hansen 1985), very few of them provide tools for the analysis of practice. Moreover, much of the literature is contentious, written to justify a particular ideological perspective (Jones and Fowles 1984).

SYSTEMS OF PRACTICE

Further, one of the difficulties with such models as do exist is that they were developed in response to particular situations, and do not therefore necessarily fit the needs of practitioners in slightly different fields or of those working for different kinds of agency. What seems to be needed is a way of looking at residential work that will enable practitioners to build their own working models of what they are doing, so that they can reflect on it and change it if they do not like what they see.

This book, therefore, cannot be about telling people *how to do it*. Residential work involves many different client groups, in many different physical settings, and many different individuals (whether as staff or as residents), and so it is not possible to generalize. What I am hoping, however, is that it will raise questions that can be answered in practical ways within the reader's own establishment. The questions are raised by attempting to look at the establishment as a working *system*, in which everything that is done is likely to have an impact on how everything else is done. On the whole, my experience is that residential workers tend to treat each person and situation as *discrete*, as separate from every other person and situation. Although this position has its virtues, particularly in its respect for the individual, it does not do justice to the complexity of the whole that makes up the residential setting. There are many reasons for thinking discretely, but I suspect that a major one is that without the proper tools it is very difficult to think in terms of wholes and the relationship between their parts. Some of the basic principles of systems thinking as they apply to residential settings are set out in the next chapter.

I suspect that one of the criticisms levelled at this book will be that it is somehow rather 'romantic'. In this context, 'romantic' means too much concern with underlying processes and feelings, without giving sufficient weight to the mundane day-to-day issues that so concern practitioners, take up so much time, and are so difficult to resolve. I plead guilty to the charge but I am unrepentant, because any real change must take place at these deep levels. Everything else is merely cosmetic. I know that the issues discussed here do not pop up in practice with convenient labels on them, but that they show themselves in innumerable specific instances that require immediate specific responses. I hope that the illustrative material will show how such general principles present themselves through practical issues. (All but a few of the illustrations are composites, in that although they are based on actual incidents, I have only used them when similar material has arisen sufficiently often to convince me that the situations are typical rather than unique. I have also taken some liberties with unimportant details to preserve anonymity and to avoid muddying the point of the illustration).

Another complaint I anticipate is that the method is not rigorous enough – the points are not proven by surveys and statistics. Such research has its place, and I shall be flattered if this work provokes some of it, but to expect it is to misunderstand the nature of the book. The ideas explored here have developed primarily out of *listening* to practitioners over many years, and trying to help them to make sense of their experience, particularly of why their best-laid plans do not always work.

The third complaint may well be that the view of residential practice is too conservative, in the light of new ideas and directions (such as those in the Wagner Report 1988). I have two thoughts on that: first, that the basic principles may still be found to apply even in the more adventurous world of very sheltered housing and normalization based on the 'most valued option' principle, and second, that we have to start from where most establishments are *now*, not where we should like them to be.

I am also conscious of many issues, which cannot be included. It may seem strange that a text concerned with values should not address itself directly to the very important political issues in residential work, such as racism and sexism in residential settings, to staff exploitation and abuse of residents, to lack of training and support for staff, to the place of residential provision within overall social policy, to issues of funding, to residents' rights, to sexuality and aggression in residence, and so on. Even this simple list is so long that it shows that such discussion requires another book of a different kind. What I do hope, however, is that the tools offered here may assist individuals to make their own more informed and sophisticated analyses of why such issues take the form that they do in the residential setting. The fact that I am not directly critical of many things that I see as undesirable practice should not be taken to mean that because I am trying to understand some of the factors that contribute to them, I am also seeking to excuse them; it simply means that this book has a different task. I hope that readers will engage in fierce debate as a result of relating the processes I describe to the above issues.

VARIETIES OF RESIDENTIAL ESTABLISHMENT

'Residential establishment' is a clumsy term. In a previous book (Atherton 1986) I tried to avoid it, and chose 'group care' as the area of analysis. I have already noted my reservations about the word 'care', but apart from that the task of that book was different, and I have chosen the boundaries of the system to suit the particular task. 'Establishment' does not pre-judge the setting by calling it a 'home', and there are occasions on which 'unit' – apart from being an even colder term than 'establishment' – needs to be kept for smaller groupings within a larger one.

'Residential establishment' implies that the major feature is that people share the same residence. They live there, and sleep there most nights. This may not be the aspect of their task that many establishments would wish to emphasize, but it must be very influential in any discussion of their social systems. Nowadays there is an immense variety of residential establishments, providing very different levels of support for their residents, and it is more difficult than it was a few years ago to detect features common to all of them. They range from those which are indeed the homes of those who live there, who do not expect to move out for the rest of their lives, to those which provide purely temporary accommodation as a respite for carers, or as a stepping stone to or from some other form of living environment. They range from those in which there is a high staffing input at all times, to those which may merely be visited by staff occasionally (it is indeed a moot point whether 'group homes' are residential establishments at all as many people understand them). Some are intimately involved with the local neighbourhood, some are isolated from it, and some are just not known by it. Some are specialized, some have a much broader base. In some the task of the staff is quite technical, involving the operation of aids and other equipment; in others the staff have only their selves and their relationships to work with. Some are merely collections of people who happen to live under one roof, and some are communities in which membership is an important feature of the lives of those who compose it. In some establishments residents pay directly for their services; in others there is no apparent connection between living there and the cost of so doing. None of these variations is 'better' than another, in absolute terms – they can only be judged by the appropriateness of their structure to their task, and the appropriateness with which the task was conceived in the first place.

With the majority of residential establishments, however, it is possible to discern a common basis to their systems which is sufficient for the analysis to be applied. These features can be enumerated thus:

1. The establishment is run according to a set of principles initially conceived by someone other than the residents. This may seem very vague, but at root it is what distinguishes a 'residential establishment' from a commune, a shared flat, or a family that employs servants. It does not distinguish it from a hotel, which shares the same basis in this respect at least.

What it means is that someone somewhere initially said, 'We need a residential establishment for such-and-such' – whether handicapped, old, or young people (see Chapter 6). The place was then set up, and even the building probably embodied certain principles that said something about the values of the originators more than those of the residents – such as having an office, or fire precautions greater than those in the average domestic house. It was staffed, and the way in which the job descriptions were defined, and the kinds of people who were recruited to fill those jobs, all developed further the values implicit in the original conception.

At last the residents came. It does not matter for this argument whether they sought the place out and chose it over others in the same market because of what it offered, or whether they were selected by the staff or the agency according to certain criteria, or both or neither. The important thing is that they came into something of a *fait accompli*. As the history of the establishment developed, the users may have modified it in many ways, but the original definition of the situation was not theirs. In a nutshell, they live there on someone else's terms.

It may well be, of course, that they like living there, and that they come to identify with the place and to see its task in the same way as the staff do. Residents are by no means necessarily oppressed. But the fundamental power distinction remains.

2. The staff and the residents therefore represent two fundamentally different groupings within the establishment. There are some therapeutic communities in which the lines are blurred between staff and residents (Kennard 1983); many of the staff may even have started off as residents, but even here there are factors that make a profound difference.

Staff are paid to work in the establishment; residents are paid for.

Staff are employed on the basis of their strengths; residents are there on the basis of their needs.

Usually, staff have an organizational hierarchy and decision-making systems; if the residents have one at all, it is an *ad hoc* one that has little continuity unless it is endorsed by the staff.

Usually staff are not there all the time; for the duration of their stay, residents spend much more time in the building and in each others' company than with the staff.

There are different standards applied to the judgement of staff behaviour and residents' behaviour; residents can 'get away with' far more. There tends in 'better' establishments (pardon the value judgement) to be a deal of concern with staff responsibilities and residents' rights; there is correspondingly less talk about staff rights and residents' responsibilities (although staff behaviour may be based on assumptions about them). While such explicit concern for residents may overall be a good thing, it does point to the extent to which residents are not judged in the same way as other fully paid-up members of our society, and to the assumption that somehow residents' rights are not the same as those of people who live outside.

Staff involvement with other members of the staff team is voluntary (in the sense that if necessary they can leave), and its intensity is diminished by its task orientation. If friendships develop between staff members, they are incidental to the performance of the task (note, however, that this was not always the case, and there may be some pockets even in the statutory sectors where husband-and-wife senior staff teams persist). On the whole, residents are lumped together on the basis of their shared needs, and it should not be thought that is necessarily a good basis for choosing the people one would want to live with. Because there is no agreed and shared task for the residents, their relationships with each other cannot be buffered by it.

3. *A residential establishment is more or less of a pressure cooker.* There are parallels to all these features in other areas of normal life. Whenever we go into a shop, onto a train, or into a pub, we are going into a situation that has been designed by someone else and which may or may not fit our expectations and interests. In all those situations, too, there are staff and there are consumers with their different roles and varying power – and on the whole such features do not matter very much. In residential settings, however, they *do* come to matter, for various reasons:

(a) Because so much interaction has to take place within the walls of the establishment; for the residents at least there is little escape. The more escape there is – whether physical or mental – the less the features matter.
(b) Because the staff and the residents spend so much time together. It is no accident that a favourite setting for

thrillers and detective stories is the country house-party, the long train journey, or a cruise. Not only is the number of suspects conveniently limited, but the limitations of space and the intimacy forced by it, and the sheer amount of interaction between those inside that space creates a hothouse or pressure-cooker effect that causes trivia to be elevated to passion.

(c) Because the residents are so tied to the staff, either in terms of physical dependence or because of the staff's control over resources or over the residents themselves. Very little can be dismissed and forgotten about.

These three conditions are sufficient to create a situation to which apply all the aspects of residential life that I shall discuss. They apply less clearly in some short-stay establishments, and in those which are minimally staffed, but they do apply insofar as there is any continuity in the life of the establishment. They certainly apply regardless of the client group, the formally designated task of the establishment, or the agency that runs it.

Interpreting Residential Life

The title of this book is carefully chosen. It refers to residential *life* because although most of the models discussed treat staff values and conduct as the major focus, the concern is with the experience of those who live in the establishment. It is about *interpreting* it because interpretation is the act of making sense of things; interpreters may translate one language into another in order that their hearers can make sense of what is being said, or performers may interpret a piece of music so that their understanding of it is conveyed to the audience. In either case, however, interpretation is a personal act: the interpreter brings to bear his own understanding and his own slant on the material in question. He uses his own frames of reference to find meaning in it. That is what I am doing here, to life in residential settings. What follows, therefore, should not be seen as the only possible interpretation. It is just one view among many, but one which will, I hope, make sense to practitioners, and enable them to see their practice in a new light. Nor am I really taking one aspect of residential life and going into progressively more depth about it, but using, as it were, a series of views from different angles to help the practitioner to get a more rounded picture of the world in which he or she works. So although most of the chapters in the book can be read on their own, and do not depend greatly on their predecessors to make sense, it is intended that they will illuminate each other.

In writing, I have had certain kinds of people in mind. First, there are senior staff who are struggling to get some kind of overall perspective on the system in which they work, and in which they themselves are engulfed. They often need a different way of looking at things in order to see the wood for the trees. I hope in some measure that while reading this they will suffer from the medical students' syndrome, of discovering that one is suffering from whatever disease the textbook is describing!

Second, there are external managers, consultants, and inspectors. They have the difficult task of trying to get to the heart of what makes a residential establishment what it is, and they rarely have enough time to do so. Often they do not seem to know what to look for, and so practitioners accuse them of concentrating on the easily assessable external features to the exclusion of the much more significant social processes. I hope that they will be provoked into asking some awkward questions.

Third, there are students and tutors. They are in the position of assembling knowledge from a number of fields, all of which illuminate residential practice in various ways, but which do not necessarily fit together. It may be presumptuous to hope that this book will provide some kind of framework within which to locate those ideas, but that is my aspiration.

Fourth, anyone who wants to know what is going on! I hope I may include some residents in this category. I write that rather sadly, because I have a vision of a resident who has read this and now sees some features of her world rather more clearly, but may still be unable to change it. It is an unfortunate reflection of reality that I have presented this list in order of the power possessed by each of the sets of people I have described.

PLAN OF THE BOOK

Chapter 1 provides a basic introduction to some of the concepts of systems thinking used in the subsequent analysis.

Chapter 2 discusses communication in the residential setting, not so much in terms of the deliberate communication procedures, but more of the unintentional communication of values carried by deeds as much as words.

Chapter 3 is about the residential establishment as a self-regulating system, and how it maintains its relatively steady state. It concentrates on first-order change and negative feedback mechanisms, and treats the day-to-day life of the establishment to all intents and purposes as a closed system. (This is a limited view, and Chapter 9 provides a corrective to it, but it is a useful starting point.)

Chapter 4 addresses itself to the question of why residential establishments function at such different levels, and proposes one answer to the question why some establishments are 'better' than others. It does so by suggesting a hierarchy of concerns in residential work analogous to the hierarchy of needs of individuals put forward by Maslow (1987).

Chapter 5 puts the steady-state ideas of the third chapter together with the questions of the fourth to explore the place of values in the form taken by practice in the establishment. It suggests one reason why some changes seem to be welcomed with open arms and to 'stick', while others meet with resistance and the system returns to the way it was before.

Chapter 6 picks up some of the ideas in previous chapters and puts them together in the notion of the 'working myth', which is rarely explicit, but embodies the practice values or theories-in-use (Argyris and Schön 1974) that dominate the life of the establishment.

Chapter 7 explores some of the working myths in practice, based on composite case-studies of various residential settings, and relates the underlying ideas to broader philosophical debates that have echoed down the centuries about human nature and the needs of people.

Chapter 8 takes just one pair of ideas that have to be balanced in practice in every residential enterprise, which I have chosen to call 'Skeleton' and 'Shell', and explores their implications both in terms of the external pressures on residential work and of the internal features of the life of the establishment.

Chapter 9 goes beyond the others, and closer to the concerns of other writers in this field, by looking at the residential establishment as an 'open' system, and what happens across rather than within its boundaries.

Chapter 10 turns to the application and implementation of the ideas, and how they might inform planned efforts towards change.

A certain amount of jargon is inevitable when one uses the systems approach, although it does not usually consist of new words, but rather of familiar ones used in unfamiliar ways: I have made an effort to keep this to a minimum without over-simplifying too much. It must be said, however, that the book is very selective in its use of material from systems thinking, and readers who want a more comprehensive account of it should turn to the bibliography. References within the text have been kept to those that shed direct light on the argument, or which show where ideas that have been mentioned in passing can be pursued in greater detail – in the case of Chapter 7 in particular this means that they are very skeletal. There is also one book that receives no direct references in the text, simply because otherwise I should be making cross-references on prac-tically every page; Douglas's *Group Living* (1986). In this book I am painting with a much broader brush than Douglas, but his amassing of the evidence from so many empirical and theoretical investigators of group relations, and his discussion of their application to residential settings is wholly complementary to the present study. He continually draws attention to the ways in which one group process may be associated with or embedded within another in residential groups; I hope that the ideas in this book will cast some light on the framework within which such embedding takes place.

A final word is in order about my own jargon. I refer to those people who live in residential establishments as 'residents', despite the limitations of the term, simply because that is the role in which they are seen in this particular study. I am very aware that they have all kinds of other qualities apart from the mere fact of where they live, and I hope that my concern with that aspect of their lives will not lead anyone to discount those other aspects that are more important. The same could be said of the use of the generalized term 'staff', which may be taken to include all those who have working contact with the residents, including cooks, domestics, and volunteers, unless otherwise stated. The meaning of 'senior staff' will vary from place to place, but should generally be self-evident. I refer to both residents and staff as 'she' or 'he'; there are more women than men in residential settings in both capacities, so perhaps I ought to stick to the female form, but variety seems preferable.

1 Systems Thinking

The systems approach appears in many guises, and it has its limitations, but here I have adopted it pragmatically in order to illuminate what seem to be some of the major issues of residential life. It is more a way of thinking about things than a body of knowledge, and it is morally neutral. That feature poses a bit of a problem, because from what I have said above it can be seen that I believe that nothing that happens in residential life is morally neutral, so the systems thinking is leavened by some discussion of values. The two go hand in hand through the argument of the book. (For a discussion of the limitations of systems thinking see Robinson 1984; for a simple introduction see Carter *et al.* 1984)

The systems approach focuses on the ways in which things, or situations, or people *relate to each other*, rather than looking at them in themselves. Take the example of Mrs Jones who is in her eighties and living with her daughter who is herself almost 60. Mrs Jones is mildly confused, cannot get about because of arthritis, and is becoming such a burden to her daughter that it may be necessary to admit her to residential care. If we see her in isolation, we shall ask a number of questions about the extent of her disability, the extent to which she may be at risk, and so on. On the basis of such questions we may make a judgement as to whether or not she is in need of support services. If on the other hand we see her in her family system, we may become aware of other issues – such as the extent to which her needs are impairing the health of her carer. But we may also find other things: it may be that some of Mrs Jones's confusion is a consequence of a lack of stimulation, and her arthritis is not of itself as severe as might be thought, but its effect is amplified by the daughter not allowing her mother to do anything for herself. This, in its turn, is not simply cruelty – and certainly not neglect – on the daughter's part. She is both worried about accidents if her mother tries to do things, and finds that the only way she can get through the day is to do things as quickly and simply as possible – which means doing things *for* her mother rather than helping her to do them for herself. Some features of the situation that previously appeared to be properties purely of Mrs Jones' physical and mental state appear in a new light. We may find, too, that Mrs Jones is acutely aware of the extent to which she is a problem for her daughter, and has therefore learned to adapt to how the daughter wants things done. The more passive, immobile, and confused Mrs Jones gets, the more her daughter has to do things for her; and the less Mrs Jones does for herself, the less capable she becomes and the more she loses touch with reality.

If we think about this simplified case a bit more, a number of features of systems thinking begin to emerge.

BOUNDARIES

There is the question of where to draw a line around the issue under discussion – in systems jargon the *boundary* of the problem. The case outlined moved the boundary from that around Mrs Jones as an individual to that around Mrs Jones-and-her-daughter. But is it appropriate to stop there? It may be that Mrs Jones' daughter works, and has made a career for herself. If she did not go out to work, leaving her mother in her chair all day with a Thermos flask and with strict instructions not to move unless she needs to go to the toilet, perhaps Mrs Jones would not be in such a state. But what difference would the daughter giving up work make to the finances? Could she cope with the strain of having no outside interests and the narrowing of her social horizons? Perhaps the appropriate boundary is Mrs Jones-and-her-daughter-and-the-daughter's-job. But is it not realistic to suggest that the whole burden of caring for Mrs Jones ought not to fall on her daughter in any case? It may be that we should be looking at Mrs Jones-and-her-daughter-and-the-daughter's-job-and-the-rest-of-the-family,   or even at Mrs Jones-and-her-daughter-and-the-daughter's-job-and-the-rest-of-the-family-and-domiciliary-support-services. But to bring in the last element is to raise questions of social policy and finance and politics, and although it may not be possible to arrive at satisfactory answers to the problems of the smaller systems without dealing with the broader ones, there is always the likelihood of losing sight of the individual case in the bigger issues.

More than this, one may raise questions about what difference it makes to the system that someone is thinking about whether Mrs Jones should be admitted to residential care. Even at the Mrs Jones-and-her-daughter level, residential provision is not simply the solution to the problem; the prospect of it – let alone its reality – may also modify the system, and thus become a part of the system (Tobin and Lieberman 1976). Mrs Jones may feel that if she goes into a Home that is the end of the road, and just give up, and die. Her daughter may feel that if residential care is the only solution she cannot commit her mother to that, and that she must soldier on. She may also wonder what she is going to do with her time when she no longer has her mother to look after; she may both look forward to the prospect and be afraid of it. All of these factors may colour the situation when a social worker comes to visit, and may affect the way in which the current problems are described to her. But the social worker is also a member of a system – an organization – and that affects both her performance and presentation of herself, and the way in which that system is perceived by the mother and daughter may be reflected in their responses to the social worker, and . . .

So it goes on. Everything in the universe is, in Arthur Koestler's term, a *holon*, that is both a part of a greater whole and itself a whole that has constituent parts (Koestler 1976). The initial question about any system is 'What are its boundaries?' How one defines the boundaries will affect very much what one sees within the system. The assumption in this book is that boundaries are generally defined too narrowly in residential social work. As suggested earlier, they tend to be drawn around individuals rather than groups, and specific incidents rather than sets of incidents, in such a way that connections are missed and opportunities for effective intervention are lost.

On the other hand, in residential work *management*, the boundaries are often drawn quite widely, to the extent that important considerations for the well-being of individuals and groups are overlooked. The manager looking for a place for a client in urgent need is likely to consult the list of vacant beds, and work from that. His frame of reference – the system with which he works – is the overall residential provision within the agency. He cannot be aware of such fine details as whether this particular person will fit in with his particular group, and hence often appears to be insensitive and autocratic when he insists that an establishment take a client when it is not ready for one, 'just because we've got a vacancy'.

Many arguments in social work theory and practice are about where the boundary should be drawn around a problem; many failures are because the 'wrong' boundary has been chosen. In this book the main boundary considered is that of the life of the residential establishment itself, as a whole. To a large extent this is also a convenient geographical boundary; we are mainly concerned with what happens inside the walls of the building (although of course there are occasions when the boundaries extend beyond that arbitrary limit). Only when we reach Chapter 9 will we go into any detail about what happens across those boundaries.

CONSEQUENCES

Let us go back to Mrs Jones and her daughter for a moment. Generally speaking, we tend to think in terms of lines of cause and effect. We might say that Mrs Jones' confusion *causes* a problem for her daughter, and that the daughter's way of dealing with her mother *causes* some of her mother's symptoms. But as the case study shows, it is not quite as simple as that: Mrs Jones' confusion is both a cause and an effect of her daughter's conduct, which is both a cause and an effect of the severity of some of Mrs Jones' symptoms. Instead of thinking in straight lines, it becomes necessary to think in circles (Fig. 1.1).

Figure 1.1 Mutual influence in Mrs Jones' household

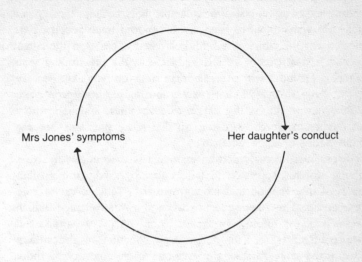

This is a *positive feedback loop*, in systems jargon. Positive feedback in this context has got nothing to do with giving people compliments; it simply means that the influence of one part of the system tends to reinforce or amplify a tendency of another part. Very often the overall consequence is a 'runaway', in which things get more and more problematic until the system breaks down altogether in one way or another. In more usual language it is a *vicious circle*.

One also finds *negative feedback loops*, and Chapter 3 is largely devoted to a discussion of negative feedback as it applies to residential settings.

For the moment the important consideration is that systems are full of such loops, and they may be said to be the characteristic feature of systems thinking. Instead of looking at a situation in terms of historical cause and effect, the systems thinker is more likely to look at it as it is now, and ask how the various parts influence each other and *keep it going as it is*.

It can be legitimately claimed that systems theorists are a little too prone to ignore the historical dimension, and therefore fail to give due weight to the extent to which people may be entrenched in positions in the system simply because those positions are what they are used to, and indeed have become part of the way in which they think of themselves. On the other hand, the past cannot be changed, and so the practitioner who is trying to find a way of changing a situation *now* may be very grateful for an insight that enables him to see how people are locked into positions in relation to each other, and hence how he might change the situation so that those positions become unnecessary or even untenable.

In practical terms, such an approach is the underlying basis of the systems approach to family therapy, and various other kinds of intervention that have grown out of the so-called Palo Alto group. They distinguish between *first-order* change, which is the kind of interaction that is going on all the time, and whose effect is to keep the overall situation in the system exactly the same, despite protestations to the contrary by those who are involved in it, and *second-order change*. First-order change is exemplified by the French saying, 'Plus ça change, plus c'est la même chose' – the more things change, the more they stay the same. Second-order change is a radical upset in the system with which the stabilizing first-order process cannot cope, and which must lead to overall change within the system, expressed in the saying, 'Things will never be the same again' (Watzlawick *et al.* 1973).

Assuming Mrs Jones' symptoms are not getting very much worse at the moment, the first-order process is that by forgetting things or dropping them or falling down or not being able to get out of bed in the morning, she confirms to her daughter that she is not capable of doing things for herself, and so the daughter does them for her. But the less she does for herself the less she is able to do, and so she forgets things (not having any responsibility for remembering them in any case), and drops them, and so on. Things are going on all the time: the daughter in particular is kept very busy, but the overall effect is that the situation remains exactly the same. If, however, the daughter became ill and was – albeit temporarily – unable to look after her mother, the cycle could not keep going. Either Mrs Jones would have to go into some kind of care, or she would have to reverse the roles and start doing at least something to look after her daughter. The latter case *might* (only 'might') bring about a permanent change in the pattern between them. If, of course, Mrs Jones tried and failed to help her daughter, that would only confirm the daughter's view of her helplessness and unreliability. But if Mrs Jones succeeded, that would create real second-order change.

The first-order/second-order change distinction is a useful one in social work in general, where a great deal of apparently change-oriented effort is in fact put into making sure that situations do *not* change, largely because of the risks involved if things go wrong. People (either clients or practitioners or both) may also have vested interests in keeping the situation the same, so that they 'raise their game' to overcome any attempts to create second-order change, exploiting the risk-reduction philosophy of social service agencies.

This focus on feedback loops and circular influences instead of straight-line causation has another feature. This is that instead of analysing the roots of behaviour or of situations, the systems perspective looks at their consequences in practice. This usually means focusing on the *function* of a particular piece of behaviour in the present situation – which may be quite different from the reasons people give for behaving in a certain way, or their expressed intentions. Mrs Jones' daughter might well explain her behaviour in terms of what she owes to the mother who did so much for her when she was a child (cause), or making sure that her mother comes to no harm (intention). Neither matters very much. What does matter is the effect of her actions in perpetuating a not entirely desirable system. It may well appear in the rest of this book that I have some harsh things to say about some well-established and well-intentioned aspects of residential practice; this is not to cast doubt on the intentions that they embody, which may be wholly laudable, but to point out that their functions are to perpetuate a system that is less than desirable. Any residential practitioner can no doubt think of several obvious examples, many of them to do with doing things *for* residents. It is difficult, for example, to explain to the well-intentioned volunteer or new member of staff in an establishment for people with a mental handicap that overall it is not desirable to help the residents with every little thing they seem to be struggling with, because otherwise they will never learn to do it for themselves. There are subtler examples, too, and it is worth being on the look-out for them.

Even so, feelings do have their part to play in the maintenance of systems. In the example, Mrs Jones' daughter would not have such an effect on her mother if Mrs Jones were not prepared to let her look after her. The 'cement' that holds the system together may be Mrs Jones' gratitude to her daughter, or perhaps her fear of her. Whether positive or negative, the emotions are an important constituent of the system, and they may indeed be one of its major determinants (Menzies 1967).

ENDS AND MEANS

This brings us back to the matter of values. All that the systems perspective can do is draw attention to the contribution that one part makes to the whole as it is functioning at the moment; it cannot make a judgement about how it *ought* to be functioning. Under the New Poor Law of 1834, workhouses were made into actively undesirable places to go into (Crowther 1983; Parker 1988). They could be discussed as systems by looking at the living conditions they offered, or the separation of husbands and wives, or other features, to see whether each part contributed to the whole; but that would not lead to any judgements about whether they were 'good' or 'bad' institutions. Similarly, one could examine the records and hazard an informed guess as to whether they did in fact deter otherwise poverty-stricken people from throwing themselves on the parish. But that would not say whether it was desirable that poor relief should be seen in that way. There is a danger with the systems perspective of believing that the ends justify the means; but all that the perspective will actually tell you is whether or not the means serve the ends. The moral judgements have to be made separately, and sometimes quite rightly take precedence over systems considerations, as we shall see later when we look at their place in residential services. I tend to agree with those people who believe that it is impossible to achieve desirable ends through undesirable means, and that if one appears to be doing so, that is only because one has drawn the system boundary too narrowly.

APPLICATION TO RESIDENTIAL SERVICES

Some readers may have wondered why I chose a case illustration that would be more likely to come to the attention of a field social worker than a residential worker. The reason was simplicity: residential work is not only a great deal more complex because of the larger numbers of people involved, but it also necessarily involves the staff as an element within the system.

One of the difficulties of investigating what happens in residential establishments is that no one knows the whole story. Despite the best efforts of staff to set up recording systems, to have change-over meetings, and to perfect their own channels of communication, the fact remains that they are not there all the time. Not only that, but they can never really enter the world of the residents and know what it is like to live in the establishment, or to live with the particular handicap or problem that brought a person there in the first place. Similarly, the residents are highly unlikely to know what it is to be a member of staff. This unavoidable ignorance operates at a number of levels; even in establishments that permit little privacy, things go on that other people do not know about first-hand. More than that, there is the issue of what events *mean* to people – for the staff, for example, Christmas may mean hard work, tensions with families and colleagues as to who works what days, and a determination to make sure that the residents have a good time. For the residents, it may mean genuine or forced jollity, bitter-sweet memories of other Christmases, or total bewilderment. Only the grossest expressions of these feelings on the part of either residents or staff ever show directly, and yet they may influence behaviour considerably. The atmosphere may be further overlaid with a strain of mutual obligation, in which the residents acknowledge how much the staff have put into the festivities, and do their best to rise to the occasion, while the staff quite reasonably expect to be repaid with just a touch of appreciation. Lest all this sound cynical, it may well be that most people do enjoy it as much as they say they do. The problem is that no one can ever know, and so everyone is forced back on interpretations – interpretations which inevitably say as much about the person doing the interpreting as that which is interpreted.

The systems approach is just as much an interpretation as any other. It does have the virtue, however, that it allows the interpreter to distance himself just a little from what is going on and from his own concerns, and to a certain extent to separate out the value judgements from the technical interpretation. I say 'to a certain extent', because one can never be wholly objective; choices of the boundary of the system under discussion, and choices about what to regard as significant and what trivial are themselves value judgements. It follows that the discussion in the rest of this book may simply say more about me than about what happens in residential establishments. Only the reader can judge that for her/himself.

2 Communication in the Residential Setting

Central to the study of systems is the part played by communication. This is really self-evident – a system consists of a number of parts, and they can only affect each other insofar as they communicate. But looked at in this light, 'communication' covers rather a wider area than it is generally believed to.

In common with most other organizations, residential services identify communication as having to do with the transfer of explicit instructions or information, up or down the hierarchy or across it. When we talk about a good communications system, we usually mean an effective way of delivering our intentional messages, whether through meetings (staff meetings or handover meetings or case conferences) or by a formal reporting system (log books, diaries, or memoranda). When things go wrong, we frequently refer to a 'breakdown in communications' – which is an effective way of not laying the blame on any particular individual. In effect, 'communication' is a 'good thing'.

The systems approach has a rather more neutral view of communication. The meaning of a communication is to be defined by its effect, and it matters little whether that effect is believed to be 'good' or 'bad':

A few years ago, one of the large voluntary child care organisations produced a film which contained scenes of two children being received at a children's home in the nineteen-fifties. They had been dressed in their best clothes for the occasion by their struggling mother. On arrival at the Home, they were immediately bustled upstairs to have a bath, and while they were in the bath, the housemother picked up their discarded clothes with a pair of tongs and dropped them into a box to be sent away for burning.

At an establishment for people with a physical handicap, staff always knock on a resident's door before entering, even when they have been summoned by the buzzer.

Neither of these examples *necessarily* means anything, but if they are taken to mean something by those at the receiving end of the communication, then they have an effect on the overall system. In any event, such individual examples may count for little in the face of other communications being received by the residents. If the staff member follows the knock with an aggressive 'What do you want *now*?' then it is likely to be dismissed by the resident as 'merely going through the motions'.

The significant thing about both examples, however, is that communication is effected by *behaviour* rather than by speech or writing. It is a commonplace to say that 'deeds speak louder than words', but the extent to which this is true is frequently under estimated in residential settings.

THE FUNCTION OF COMMUNICATION

Systems theory answers the basic question about why things are the way they are by concentrating not so much on the original causes of a situation, but on how it continues to be as it is. Original causes are part of this, but only insofar as they continue to be influential in the minds of people in the present situation, or in the rules that govern it. To take a simple example:

Many years ago, there was a power cut one Friday at a residential school for emotionally disturbed children. Because there was no hot water or cooking facilities, the staff sent out for fish and chips which the children ate out of the paper bags. They enjoyed this variation from the normal meal-time routine so much that it became a normal procedure for Friday lunch, although the meal was cooked on the premises. Nowadays, few of the staff remember how this routine came to be, but they continue to operate it. They do so not merely because of history (although a sense of continuity is quite important), but because it provides variety and informality and a marker for the approaching end of the school week.

In this benign example, it is the part played by the messages given by fish and chips in the *present* system that is important: this particular establishment is perfectly capable of changing when it needs to. On the other hand:

In an elderly people's home which faces onto a busy road, a resident given to wandering had once walked out onto the road and had been knocked down. This prompted the management to install a remote-controlled lock on the front door which was operated from inside the office. (It was de-activated if the alarm went off.) No residents had been inclined to 'wander' onto the road since its installation, but it continued to be used: it worked as an excellent rationalization for controlling the movements of residents, and also perhaps as an excuse for senior staff to 'have to' be in the office all the time.

Here, the original dubious justification was also almost forgotten, but could be trotted out as an excuse if the residents wanted to know why they were locked in. The system could easily have been abandoned, but it served the purposes of the staff too well for that.

At this point the reader may feel that we are not discussing communication, but structural features of the organization of the residential setting. The reply is that all such features are forms of communication, and are much more difficult to ignore than simple verbal or written messages. Some evidence for this is provided by the reaction of the residents in the old people's home: soon after the installation of the remote lock, they gave up going straight to the door, and would first tap on the glass of the reception counter to be recognized and to be 'allowed ' out. It is indeed possible that even if the lock were disconnected, they would continue to act in the same way. All effective connections between elements in the system are forms of communication, although the content of the message may have to be inferred from its consequences.

HIDDEN MESSAGES

In educational circles there is the concept of the 'hidden

curriculum' (first coined by Snyder 1971). This refers to what people learn by virtue of the system of education to which they are exposed, regardless of the intentions of the staff as to what they should learn. An emphasis on examinations, for example, may teach that learning is only to be valued in terms of the qualifications, which may follow; and the labelling procedures of schools may tell some pupils that they are written off by the establishment regardless of what they do.

What we are examining here is the equivalent of the hidden curriculum. For some people it is suggested that admission to residential provision in the first place is such a powerful communication about their incapacity or troublesomeness that it can never be overcome (see 'Across the Boundaries', p. 176). For others the experience of life in a residential setting can be either positive or negative depending on the hidden messages that they pick up. Such messages also tend to be assimilated into self-fulfilling or self-defeating prophecies; eventually people come to accept that they are indeed what the staff believe them to be, although there are always some determined characters who set out to prove them wrong. If residential establishments are powerful in no other respect, they have a great capacity for affecting the self-image of those who live in them.

It is usually the structure of the routine procedures that conveys the powerful messages, although of course the manner of the staff and what they say to each other out of the hearing of the residents (and perhaps of the senior staff) is also potent. Routines, however, are institutionalized reflections of the values of the establishment, and their sheer repetition is bound to get through to most residents eventually. Such procedures include 'backstage' routines such as those of the office and the laundry room as much as the visible 'front of house' activity (Goffman 1971):

In a children's home, the office (although still known as such), had become virtually another sitting room, and was frequently used by the young people for peace and quiet while the record-player or the TV were on in other rooms. The only concession to its office status was that the room was locked when there were no staff in. As a member of staff commented, 'People do not have offices in their own homes, where decisions are made about their lives and records are kept without them knowing about them. So although we need a room for the records and the like, we try to de-mystify it as much as possible.'

In an old people's home, there was considerable concern on the part of some residents about the laundry. Some of them did not like the idea of their clothes being washed together with those of incontinent residents, and so quite an elaborate system had to be set up to re-assure them: not only was such mixed washing not to be done, it also had to be *seen* not to be done.

The challenge for staff is to work out which messages are important to residents, because the experience of living in a residential setting can lead people to have unusual priorities. Issues that would be mere irritations in the outside world can assume enormous proportions within the confines of the establishment, while others can be ignored. Moreover, 'little things' can stand for much larger ones, especially when the residents concerned are not particularly articulate:

When asked how he liked a long-stay children's home in comparison with the assessment centre from which he had moved, a not-very-bright boy thought for quite a long time before saying that he preferred this place, because here there was a choice of cereals for breakfast.

Clearly there was more to it than the boy revealed – the assessment centre would not have become like the children's home just by introducing a choice of cereals, but that element of choice symbolized for him all the differences in approach to the young people. In time, others might come to light.

TRUST AND RISK

Perhaps the major issue communicated in this way is the degree of trust the staff have in the residents. This is not always 'trust' in a moral sense, but also trust in their capabilities. Making sure that all medication is held in the office or medical room, kept under lock and key in a special cabinet, and doled out at the appropriate times by the senior staff, says effectively that residents cannot be trusted to look after and take their own medication as they would at home. Locking anything up, indeed, gives a message about lack of trust, although it is not always lack of trust of the resident (Cameron 1988). Locking up at night, for example, may enable everyone to sleep more soundly because the outside world cannot always be trusted. I would be the last to deny that locks and safeguards of this kind are sometimes very necessary, but that fact should not blind us to the implications of the procedures, since after all there is no prima facie reason why moving to live in an old people's home should mean that someone is incapable of handling her own medication (Wagner 1988).

A similar issue attaches to access to residents' rooms, to procedures for handling their money, and so on. With active residents, including young people, there is the issue of being accompanied when going out, or the monitoring of relationships. The reasons may all be stated in terms of the reduction of risk, but there is a problem in drawing the line between being realistic about risks for the sake of the resident, and being over-cautious from the point of view of come-backs on the staff. This issue also comes up in the discussion of the residential establishment as a self-regulating system (Chapter 3).

OVER-SENSITIVITY

It may be suggested that such concerns betray a degree of academic over-sensitivity. Many residents, it is claimed, have never known anything very different because their youth or their disability has always meant that others have assumed responsibility for them even before admission. In the case of people with a mental handicap it is often believed that they are not capable of understanding the covert messages conveyed by the system in any case.

We need to be wary of taking such a line, partly because the argument can be used to deny civil rights and erode the quality of life of residents even further, and partly because where the messages are about relationships, they come through very clearly regardless of the ability of the recipient to spell out exactly what they mean. Bateson (1973), who did a great deal of work on animal communication, points out that the most basic forms of communication are those concerned with relationships, rather than about 'third-party' issues or information about objects other than the sender and the recipient. The cat rubbing itself up against your legs as you open the fridge door is not giving a message that could be translated into language as, 'Please feed me,' but is conveying a much more general statement about the nature of the relationship between the two of you that may best be expressed as 'dependence', or – rather more anthropomorphically – as 'I depend on you'.

DIGNITY

Looked at in this light, all actions in a residential setting contribute to the maintenance or erosion of a sense of dignity on the part of the residents, and it must be admitted that such a sense is very difficult to preserve under the circumstances. Adolescents in care have often had any pretensions towards dignity (or in old-fashioned language, 'self-respect'; in new language, a 'positive self-image') knocked out of them by previous circumstances. People with a mental or physical handicap have frequently been so stigmatized by their previous experience that they may not even know what dignity is; and old people frequently feel humiliated by their inability to do for themselves what they were able to do without thinking for so many long years.

As Maslow's hierarchy of needs (see p. 61 for more details) indicates, to talk of dignity or self-esteem may be meaningless to people who are preoccupied by lower-order needs, but that does not excuse those responsible for other people's lives from making every effort to provide an environment within which dignity can grow, if at all possible.

WHAT COMMUNICATION IS POSSIBLE

If we put the preceding ideas together with those about the establishment as a self-regulating system (see Chapter 3) and the potency of administrative convenience (Chapter 5), it becomes clear that within any given setting it is possible to say or otherwise communicate some ideas that are readily heard, while others do not 'get through' no matter how loud one shouts. As a general rule we can say that *only those messages that are consistent with the overall culture or working myth* (Chapter 6) *of the establishment will be heard*.

(As suggested in the other sections referred to, we can therefore tell quite a lot about the culture of the establishment by looking at those messages that are heard and those that are not).

Technically, communication is only possible when the level of the signal is sufficiently strong to be distinguished from the surrounding *noise*. (Specifications for radios and tape recorders, for example, refer to their 'signal-to-noise ratio'.) Noise is anything that is irrelevant to the message being transmitted, and it may in fact be another, interfering message (such as a crossed telephone line). In the residential setting, there are so many channels of communication – ranging from the design of the building through the procedures to fleeting facial expressions on the part of individuals – that when they reinforce each other, the signal level is extremely high, and such messages are perfectly capable of drowning out any other attempts at communication that are not consistent with them. The major way in which such reinforcement of messages takes place is through back-up procedures.

Similarly, where one deliberate message is contradicted by others, the signal is drowned out by the overall noise level, and the communication is ineffective. Improving the signal-to-noise ratio is not merely a matter of making the signal louder, but also of reducing the noise level. Unless action is taken on both fronts, all that is likely to be achieved is the creation of mixed messages, as discussed below.

Redundancy

Back-up procedures are examples of redundancy. We normally use this word to describe people losing their jobs because they are surplus to requirements in a company, but the present usage is borrowed from linguistics (Cherry 1980: 117ff) where – when one examines it – the meaning is not so very different. Redundancy in jobs implies that there is more than one person doing work that could be done by one person; there is duplication of effort. Redundancy in communication means (roughly) that the (communication) system does not rely on merely one way of getting its message across. It uses complex patterning so that even if the message is distorted and some of the information content is lost, it may still make sense. Agreement of subject and verb, word order, and emphasis and intonation in spoken language all tend to carry the same message in different ways; we may regard language as similar to a rope made up of many fibres, each individually weak but together almost unbreakable.

In the system of the residential establishment too, there is a great deal of redundancy. Relations between senior and junior staff, for example, may be characterized not only by formal authority, but also by greater experience and perhaps expertise on the part of the seniors, *and* by comfortable social relations, *and* by a shared history of working together, and by other features. Take any one or even two away, and the system will still operate. Hygiene is ensured not only by the activity of the domestic staff, but *also* by procedures followed by the professional staff, *and* expectations of residents, *and* by the design of the facilities and equipment that may be at risk of contamination by germs, *and* by special procedures when there is a known risk of infection, and so on.

Although such redundancy means that disasters rarely happen, it can also mean that positive change is difficult to institute, because the contribution of some of the elements to the performance of a task may not immediately be obvious. This is particularly the case when we come to the less tangible elements of the culture of the establishment. In recent years, for example, efforts have been made in many establishments to make them more 'homely', but such efforts have been vitiated time and again by many of the features mentioned earlier in this chapter. The design of the building shouts 'institution' – fire precautions are necessary; the furniture has to be designed to take harsher punishment than at home; furnishings must be easily cleanable; domestics and a cook have to be employed – not to mention the professional staff who come and go off duty and have to be paid to work there. Against such strong mutually reinforcing messages, the different-coloured candlewick bedspreads and the pictures on the lounge walls make little impression.

Redundancy can be used to advantage, however, when all aspects of the living environment are consciously designed to reinforce the same messages:

In a programme of 'ordinary housing' for people with a mental handicap, committed to principles of normalization, the basic guideline for purchasing was that all appliances (cooker, fridge, washer, etc.) should be ordinary domestic models, on the grounds that anything else would not be consistent with the philosophy of the programme.

It is not uncommon in homes for elderly people to encourage them to bring in with them as much of their own furniture as their rooms will allow, because of the memories and continuity symbolized by it.

In a therapeutic community for adolescents, an extensive programme of re-furbishment was carried out, based on the assumption that *everything* in the establishment carried messages for the young people about their worth, and about genuineness. Amongst other things, this meant not using any artificial fibres in the soft furnishings.

In another rather different unit for young people, there was a cellar which they themselves had painted in violent and dark colours. It seemed to stand for their underlying feelings of violence, hate and fear. An effort was therefore made by the staff to create a light and airy sitting-room at the top of the house, decorated in subtle pastels, to show that the 'other side' of the residents was also acknowledged and to encourage its expression.

MIXED MESSAGES

These examples are of physical surroundings, and it is at this level and that of formal procedures that redundancy is most often found at its strongest (consider the formal back-up procedures for checking the administration of medication). At the level of relationships, the differentiation between staff and resident roles also tends to be characterized by redundancy (staff are paid, residents paid for; staff go off duty, residents stay there; staff have privacy, residents do not; and so on); but the specialization of staff roles means that at the level of personal rather than structural relationships with residents, there is much less multiplication of communication channels.

In the 'outside world' those who care for others tend to have other relationships with them that provide an overall rationale for their activity – usually family relationships. Moreover, they do practically everything necessary for the person they care for. The paradigm case is that of the mother with her child. She feeds him, dresses him, bathes him, changes him, plays with him, cuddles him, trains him, protects him, and scolds him. Most discrepant messages, such as her anger when he is naughty, can be seen in the context of this overall care, and so the child develops an understanding of the relationship based on the major signals, which swamp the contrary ones (hence the notion of the 'good-enough' mother; Winnicott 1980) Things can go wrong with this pattern, of course, as in the case of the 'double bind' (Bateson 1973).

In the residential setting, relationships with staff are much more tenuous, and therefore more vulnerable to mixed messages.

In a unit for adolescent girls, the staff's declared attempts to get them to believe in their own worth and value were undermined by the cook, who obviously believed them to be the dregs. She expressed this by the casual way in which she prepared the food and careless presentation. However, as important as her own message was that of the rest of the staff who did not challenge her on her attitude, or attempt to improve the situation by showing that they valued meal times. One part of an attempt (ultimately unsuccessful) to turn the culture round had to address itself to the cooking and presentation of food.

(Food, of course, is a very potent communication because of its symbolic significance as well as its practical importance. See Beedell 1970 and Berridge 1985).

Residential establishments are also breeding grounds for mixed messages, which leave the recipients confused and unable to respond effectively. Characteristically, such mixed messages are conveyed when there is a formal policy that espouses one value, but the inclination of the staff and the active working myth is in a different direction, or where the staff use them in order to confuse authority issues.

At the level of staff behaviour, the commonest mixed message (and one that is very difficult for other staff to confront) is that of 'I'm only obeying orders', in which the letter of a procedure is followed but not the spirit. Then there is the mixed message that might be acceptable in the context of the greater redundancy of relationships in the outside world, but is confusing within the residential setting. One common form of this is the 'joking' or bantering relationship, which is frequently adopted by staff in order to confuse the issue of their power. It is often a matter of intonation rather than words used, and therefore difficult to illustrate on the printed page, but in its extreme form may include 'friendly' insults: 'Come on, you old fool, it's time for your bath!' (to a deaf old gentleman who is alleged not to be able to hear anyway); or 'jokey' orders: 'Look, Mrs Jones, you've got to eat *something*! If you don't, I shall just have to leave you here until you do, shan't I?' The resident cannot argue with such communication – if he or she protests, the staff member brushes it off by claiming she was only joking, and can the resident not take a joke? In the first example, the resident could also be accused of feigning deafness rather than really being unable to hear. If the resident obeys orders, as it were, then the communication has had its desired effect, so the staff member 'wins' both ways.

The difficulty for the resident is that she or he does not have enough experience of the staff member to know how to 'take' (or to 'frame') the message (Goffman 1975). Is it a joke, or is it real? If for any reason understanding is difficult – because of deafness, or poor sight to make sense of non-verbal accompanying messages, because of intellectual limitations or emotional disturbance, or simply because of an appreciation of the overall power of the staff – the message may be taken much more literally than it is meant. The overall effect is to de-skill residents and to reinforce their dependence; Bateson goes so far as to suggest that the common social work term 'ego-strength' is to be understood in terms of the ability of a person to assign a message to its appropriate category, that is how it is to be 'taken'.

A similar 'double-bind' or catch-22 is set up by patronizing tones: 'Now, we can't leave this bedroom in this state, can we? We're supposed to be learning to be independent, aren't we?' The message of the words is about being independent, the message of the phrasing and intonation is about being dependent.

Such double messages prohibit reasoned objections by those who receive them; the only option for the frustrated resident is often to strike out either verbally or physically, which results in them being labelled 'difficult' or 'cantankerous' or 'disturbed'.

Teasing is a part of the socialization process through which individuals learn to frame messages and make sense of relationships. It sometimes drives young children to tears of frustration, but for people who are traumatized or unsure of their position, it is even worse. They are only going to be able to show their true capacities, and learn to have any trust at all in those on whom they are dependent, if the messages they receive are 'straight', or consistent on all levels. As far as I can see, the *only* exception to this is the use of gentle and carefully monitored teasing as part of the process of preparing people to manage in the outside world, where they are likely to encounter such mixed messages, including sarcasm and irony.

COMMUNICATIONS FROM RESIDENTS

We have discussed communication so far in terms of messages from the staff to the residents. Naturally there are messages in the opposite direction: residents who are consistently incapable of acting in conformity with staff expectations, for example, are telling the staff that they have to act differently. These messages do not always get across as effectively, because on the whole the residents have less power than the staff. Thus the previously continent old person who becomes incontinent may be interpreted as 'doing it out of spite' for a long time before the nature of the problem is recognized. Similarly, the resident who 'improves' and wishes to assert herself may not be heard, and her behaviour may be reinterpreted as further evidence of her original 'problem'. Such 'looping' is a useful way for staff to discount the messages coming from residents, and finds its most complete expression where residents have already been labelled as 'mad', 'disturbed', or 'confused' (Goffman 1968).

Such conduct is often labelled as 'attention-seeking'. Seeking attention is the most natural thing in the world, particularly when one is not assured of it on demand (Steiner 1975). There are of course some people whose need for constant emotional attention is insatiable, because of previous experiences. But for many people in residential settings, the need to seek attention and to indulge in behaviour that gets it (usually in a negative form) is as much a creation of the establishment as of the individual. The underlying question is, 'What do you have to do to get noticed in here?' The answer is all too frequently that you have to appeal to the establishment at the most basic level of its concerns, either at the physical and safety levels or at the order level, and so that is what residents do.

The added ingredient in communication that residents lack but staff have is *power*. This does not simply mean force, but the control of elements of the system that cannot be ignored because the residents are dependent on them. In the case of locked doors, for example, it is ultimately the physical strength of the door and the lock that confers power on the staff:

A girl was being admitted to a newly-built secure unit. She was understandably not very happy about the process, and when she was shown her 'room' (or cell), she slammed the door behind her as hard as she could. The door held, but the frame began to come away from the wall. The staff member noticed this before the girl did and hastily ushered her to another room.

Whether the message of the physical security was a 'good' one or a 'bad' one, it would clearly have lost much of its impact had the girl realized that she was stronger than the building.

But this incident illustrates another principle: that the staff often do not understand the messages they are communicating. Only the girl ultimately knew whether the locks on the doors and the discreet bars on the windows meant oppressive incarceration or the re-assurance that here was an environment that could contain the chaos and destructiveness and turmoil that she felt inside. The messages may well have been different for different girls in the unit, and different for the same girl at different times. But since staff are not always aware of sending the messages, they have little clue as to what they mean. They are baffled by the derision with which their sincere expressions of care and concern are greeted by residents, or sometimes by the apparently unwarranted appreciation expressed for merely routine activity.

Individual communications have to be assessed in the context of the whole, and on the whole it is the residents who get a more complete picture. This is partly because they are there for longer than the staff, partly because the establishment is their home (even temporarily), partly because they may have fewer distractions (it is worth noting how many physical features of residential settings go unnoticed by active adolescents), and partly because they are dependent.

PROJECTION AND SPLITTING

There remains one further major dimension of communication to be covered in this brief overview of the issues – unconscious processes. I have briefly discussed linking and transference as they apply to residential settings elsewhere (Atherton 1986), and there is an enormous psychoanalytic literature on the subject (for a good introduction see Sandler, Dare, and Holder 1979).

This is not the place to discuss the validity of the concept of the unconscious, particularly as it applies to group processes. For the moment suffice it to say that the hypothesis of unconscious processes seems to be the most useful one for explaining some strange phenomena that undoubtedly do occur in residential and other group settings.

Perhaps the clearest illustration is what has come to be known in management and supervision courses as the 'there's always one' phenomenon. Practically every residential establishment seems to have its problem staff member whose approach to the job seems to undermine that of everyone else. Such staff members may be scapegoated by others, especially outside the establishment; within it they may not even be confronted. Frequently, however, the issue is not merely with the staff member herself. If she is moved to another establishment, for example, she may act quite differently. This suggests that she has a role to play within the overall culture of the establishment, embodying values that other staff may feel but are not able to express or even acknowledge to themselves. They 'project' such feelings onto her and can thereby deny them in themselves (Klein 1958; Main 1975). From the point of view of change, the issue is that she is not going to be able to change until the other staff take back their projections and allow her to.

The residential setting is a fertile medium for the growth of the projection and its associated mechanisms of introjection and splitting. In the latter case, different people or parts of the system come to represent values or feelings that are conflicting in an unresolved way in the whole group, and the subsequent struggle between those parts of the system (if the split is not contained by them) is like a fight of champions on behalf of a confused populace who do not seem to know whom to support:

A young member of staff arrived at a hostel for people with a mental handicap. She had no previous experience in social work, but was academically well qualified. She acknowledged that she knew little about the work. At first she was taken under the wing of the Head of Home, who was unqualified but had years of experience and was nearing retirement. The Head ran the hostel with relatively benign paternalism, but would tolerate no disagreement with his views or methods, which led to a subculture of resentment (and even fear) amongst the rest of the staff. As the new arrival began to learn the ropes, and used her academic skill to broaden her knowledge of mental handicap, she began to make suggestions for change in the directions of normalization. These were dismissed, but she slowly became aware that she was being 'set up', as she put it, to oppose the Head of Home at all times, although she soon found that she could not rely on the backing of other staff who had appeared to egg her on. The situation became increasingly strained until she left to go on a qualifying course.

Conflict over working myths may also express itself through such mechanisms (see Chapter 6).

Projection and splitting appear in resident groups, where they may be combined with the labelling of residents by others and by staff to force them to carry delinquency, confusion, self-destructiveness, or sexuality on behalf of others. Occasionally they also carry the hopes of others in terms of 'progress', whatever that means within the particular context. It often appears that people in this position already carry in themselves the germ of what they later come to represent, but the amplification caused by projection can be very dangerous, particularly if it begins to have secondary consequences such as court appearances or suicide attempts that affect the later course of the person's life.

The field of such projections can also be between the staff and resident groups, sometimes creating a collusive mutual projection in which the staff represent all the strength and the residents all the weakness and need (endemic in Shell structures; see Chapter 8).

A similar mechanism lies at the root of the reflection process, the classic form of which has been observed in authoritarian establishments where the subculture among the residents holds up a bizarre mirror to the relations between the staff and the residents (Polsky 1965; Wills 1971). It may take other forms, however, with the staff acting out the problems of the residents, or vice versa:

A hospice is the kind of setting where it may be expected that there would be very strong feelings. In one such establishment which had not fully worked through some of these feelings, it was felt important to preserve the atmosphere of calm for the dying patients. The patients obliged, and appreciated the serenity of their environment: but they still had unresolved feelings of rage at their fate, and these were projected into the staff, who were unable to contain them, but whose relationships were characterized by bitterness and fragmentation.

Or the split may be between the internal world of the establishment and the outside world, making the one all good at the expense of the other, which becomes all bad, perhaps building on the conflict between security and freedom.

Projection and introjection and splitting are rather mysterious processes. They do not always occur, and many group roles are largely independent of them. Individuals *do* have personal characteristics that may set them apart or create friction, but unconscious mechanisms need to be considered when the power of the feelings engendered seem disproportionate to the issues that give rise to them, and perhaps when the experience of trying to resolve the problems indicates that those concerned would rather have the problem than its solution. As in the case of distorted family systems, the projection serves the felt interests of the majority of the group at the expense of a few of its members. It is also possible that when such issues have been around for a long time, they will have had their effect in the formal procedures and policies of the establishment, as well as in its informal culture (Menzies 1967). For those taking on management responsibility, such problems are fairly intractable even when recognized, but above all they demand that the problem not be located simply in the object(s) of the projections, but also in the group as a whole.

3 The Residential Establishment as a Self-Regulating System

One of the significant features of residential work is that much of it takes place within the confines of four walls. This simple fact has strange consequences: at work one can feel that only what happens within those walls is real, and the outside world is a kind of distant fantasy. This is particularly the case when, for one reason or another, the worker does not set foot outside the establishment for twenty-four hours or more. She blinks as she emerges into the light, and sometimes seems surprised that the rest of the world is still there.

The isolation of the residential worker's little world is less of an issue now than it was in the days before defined working weeks, when many staff lived on the premises as well, but it can still feel very different from the 'normal' world. One consequence is that perspectives can become distorted. The trivial can become magnified into something major, and things that really matter outside can pale into insignificance. Heads of Home have been known to develop delusions of grandeur, and to treat their domain as if it were a self-contained empire. Staff sometimes become obsessed with matters that simply do not make sense to outsiders, and find it hard to muster any interest in even those external issues that affect their own interests.

This overall perspective treats the establishment as a closed system – as something set apart from the real world and relatively unaffected by it. If it affects staff, it can affect residents even more strongly. It becomes difficult to see the establishment as simply part of something wider, and anyone who has the temerity to take such a view is seen as insensitive and dismissive of the hard work and commitment that go into making the place work – which often means that the agency management cannot win.

I have described this temporary institutionalization syndrome as if it were a bad thing, but perhaps it is necessary in some measure. It seems to take a pathological form particularly in some elderly people's homes, largely because the residents do not go outside much, and hence staff do not get out of the building and because they are long-stay 'homes' – but it is also to be found in other establishments, where it is a side effect of the commitment of the staff to the residential community. It is dangerous and destructive when it gets out of hand, but in a minor form it has its virtues.

Those virtues lie in the commitment, or more technically in the concern to hold the boundary between the internal world of the establishment and the environment. Although there are respects in which openness to the environment is important, and indeed some designs of residential establishment in which it is a corner-stone, nevertheless preservation of the 'differentness' of culture can be a useful way of communicating to the staff and the residents that they are cared about. It is no accident that in many establishments where there is a feel of a distinctive culture, of a distinctive 'standing-for-something' about the place, there is also *as a side effect* a degree of tension between the members of that culture – the 'insiders', be they staff or residents – and the 'outsiders', including the management of the agency that runs the establishment. I emphasize that this comes as a side effect. I know of other places where there is a similar tension, but it does not represent anything about the quality of what is going on inside, merely failure of communications and understanding. Simply to aim at the creation of tension is self-destructive.

At one child-care establishment, there was a history of relatively minor overspending on the food budget, and the Department would frequently ring up to query the purchase of what the bureaucrats saw as unwarranted exotic food purchases, such as fresh pineapple (even when this was actually cheaper than the tinned equivalent). The residents probably had no idea that it was going on, apart from the odd occasions when they compared notes with children from other places and found that the food was better at their own establishment. Nevertheless, there was a little fight going on between the senior staff and the

Department, in which the staff were effectively saying that the residents were worth more than the Department was prepared to spend on them, and this contributed to a culture of the staff 'being on the side of the kids', which was generally beneficial to the life of the establishment as a whole.

In various meetings with residential staff, the question has come up of the tyranny of the telephone. Whenever the 'phone goes, it *has* to be answered, and senior staff have to drop everything in order to respond to the immediate problem raised by whoever is ringing up. In discussion, it is clear that such immediate attention is not accorded to the staff's own telephone queries to management or anyone else: in system terms the effect is that anyone ringing up can effectively 'take over' the establishment by demanding an immediate response, and the boundary is not being held. Staff are frequently horrified at the thought that they might be unavailable and that someone might merely take a message, but become aware of the extent to which dropping everything for the 'phone devalues the chat with the resident or the supervision session or whatever else is in progress at the time.

It is a necessary fiction for the therapeutic development of an establishment that in some respects what happens inside is 'better' than the outside world. This can of course go over the top, so that all the goodness and care and warmth are to be found within, and all the badness and neglect and coldness to be found outside, so that residents are frightened of ever straying away from the safety of the nest (see Chapter 2). But in its positive form it can account for the optimism that is often characteristic of experimental establishments or those that are run independently – after all, if one is in the market-place, it is clearly necessary to believe that what one is selling is better than the competition or better than nothing. There is a feeling that 'in here we are doing something useful', 'in here we have something to offer'. Where this positive evaluation is lacking, staff and resident morale tends to be low, and there is therefore little chance of the experience of residence being in any sense beneficial to those who live there.

The differential between the internal world of the establishment and the culture of the external world can take many forms, and these will be taken up further in the discussion of working myths (Chapter 6). Some of them are not really to the benefit of the residents, but simply serve to maintain some sense of identity for the staff. Some assessment centres for young people, for example, used to pride themselves on the 'professionalism' of their assessment reports, consisting of many pages of documentation from staff and practitioners of other disciplines. This may have helped the staff to feel good, but tended to create an image of the young people as experimental animals, being put through hoops and sorted and labelled. However, it is easy to see that in an establishment with a constant through-put of young people, where relationships tended to be fairly distant, and where recommendations were in practice not often acted upon, the assessment report was probably the only bit of the task in which the staff could take any pride.

The above discussion has implied a number of different forms of boundary between the internal world of the establishment and the outside. There is a physical form, represented by the walls of the building or the limits of the grounds surrounding it; there is a cultural form, to do with the different values held internally and externally; and there is a task form, determined by what the establishment was set up to do by those who organized it. All three interact – the design and constraints imposed by the building may follow the task, and the task (as in the case of the assessment centres mentioned above) may influence the culture, just as the culture may reach back and modify the task-in-practice as opposed to the original aim. However, the nature of the day-to-day work of the establishment tends to focus attention on the physical and cultural boundaries to the exclusion of the task – and it is this which leads to thinking in terms of a closed system.

ON CLOSED SYSTEMS .

Talk of something as a 'closed system' is generally taken as abuse, rather like a 'closed mind'. People sometimes refer to closed systems of thought, like psychoanalysis or Marxism, that are so all-encompassing that they have the capacity to explain away objections to them within their own framework (Berger 1961). Or the phrase may be used to define institutions that are not open to change, and in which roles are fixed (Jones 1978). Such evaluations are not implied here, where the phrase is being used in a technical sense to direct attention to what happens within the boundaries of the establishment, without regard to the influences and demands of the outside world. It must be emphasized that this is purely a convenience for the sake of the present discussion. The only closed system in existence is the universe as a whole – and if one believes in God, even that is debatable. Every part of that universe is an open system (technically a subsystem or *holon*), because it is subject to the influence of its environment. What I am doing in this discussion is similar to what the practitioners referred to above do, that is leave the outside world out of account for the moment.

The value in residential work that a computer scientist would refer to as the 'default value' (*i.e.* the value to which the system returns unless made to do otherwise) is 'the smooth running of the establishment'. That is to say, practically every residential worker, whatever her other values or orientations, likes to see the internal world of the establishment ticking over smoothly, without crises or hiccups. This is of course very rare, but it remains the value held in most minds, and it appears to motivate much of the work that goes on inside the establishment. (There are occasional exceptions to this rule, mainly in the field of therapeutic communities, where crises are the fuel on which they run; but anyone acquainted with such communities will be aware that with certain changes, the following observations also apply to them.)

In itself, there is nothing wrong with trying to get the establishment to run smoothly; indeed, it may well be the prerequisite for any other kind of social work intervention to be offered to the residents (see Chapter 4). As we shall see, it can become a problem when it takes precedence over all else, but several features flow from it.

Minimizing Risk

Anyone trying to design any system that is intended to run smoothly, whether social or mechanical or electrical, knows the importance of back-up or fail-safe devices. These are features that are incorporated so that if one thing goes wrong, the system can continue to cope or the damage to it is at least contained. Most cars have dual braking systems, in which even if the hydraulic pressure is lost in the footbrake, the hand-brake cable system will still slow the car down and eventually stop it. Electrical circuits have fuses, so that if something goes wrong with an appliance or the whole circuit is overloaded, only the fuse blows, and the danger of shocks or fires is minimized.

In the same way, residential establishments are characterized by their back-up systems, so that occurrences that would cause problems in a 'normal' domestic setting are anticipated, and equipment and procedures are available for dealing with them. Such systems are part of the redundancy in the establishment (see page 33). Some of these back-up systems are visible, such as fire-fighting equipment – and indeed the necessity for their installation (as decreed by fire departments and management) can militate against the creation of a domestic atmosphere in places like group homes. The house may superficially look like all the others in the street, and there may be only four people living there, but only this house has a fire escape, self-closing fire-stop doors, and a sprinkler system. There is a delicate balance to be achieved between domesticity and the avoidance of risk. There may also be first-aid and medicine cabinets that are more comprehensively equipped than in any domestic home, and locks on more doors. Less visibly, there may well be procedures to deal with potential emergencies or crises, some of which become routinized. If a young person runs away from home in the 'normal' world, it is a cause of great stress and anxiety and maybe much heart-searching before the police are involved; in an adolescent unit there is likely to be a rule as to when 'abscsonsions' need to be reported, and a form to fill in for the police to collect. Only very rarely are people 'sectioned' under the Mental Health Act from the community at large. In a hostel for recovering mentally ill people the numbers of the G.P., the local mental hospital, and the emergency duty team from Social Services are posted next to the office telephone. One of the greatest crises of all for most people is encountering the death of another person; in the elderly persons' home, what to do and whom to inform is set out in the procedures manual.

Crises, then, are catered for. In some measure they are routinized. A death is never easy to come to terms with; a compulsory admission to hospital raises slightly less powerful feelings; an absconsion may simply be irritating (for staff). Less attention may be given to helping staff and other residents to cope with their feelings about such an incident than to ensuring that all the proper procedures are carried out so that the establishment as a whole can carry on functioning as if nothing had happened. It is difficult to rock the boat of a residential establishment. Most eventualities have been foreseen, particularly the bad ones. (The establishment may find it more difficult to cope with a proposed marriage between two residents in an old people's home – even more so in a hostel for people with mental or even physical handicaps – or a bright adolescent studying for university entrance.)

It is debatable how desirable it is that the system should be unshockable. In some circumstances continuity and security are more important than others, and an inappropriate emphasis on them helps to create a Shell environment (see Chapter 8). But this development of procedures for the management of crises and the avoidance of risk points to a number of features of the closed system:

1. On the whole such procedures are not questioned. This lack of questioning indicates an implicit acceptance on the part of staff and management that the values of the residential establishment *must* be different from those of the environment. The occasions on which they *are* questioned are generally those on which they are felt to be inadequate.

2. Their existence points to a priority given in the structure of the establishment to the minimization of disturbance.

Just as an ocean liner has stabilizers, the residential establishment must be able to ride out storms without those within it being unduly affected.

3. It also suggests that the staff as much as the residents should be preserved from the full impact of unusual events, and that these events can be treated as essentially similar in nature. An absconsion may be because the young person was running away from the unit or running to someone else, or a combination of both; this makes little difference to the procedures.

Prescriptive Thinking

The existence of redundant procedures and the general concern to see that the establishment runs smoothly have an effect on the outlook of practitioners in residential work. Broadly, this is a tendency towards what may be termed 'prescriptive thinking'. It would require fairly specialized research to work out whether residential work attracts people who are prescriptive in their outlook in the first place, or whether experience in the work makes them so, or whether – as is most probable – it is a combination of the two. In any event, a prescriptive approach to a situation is one that concentrates immediately on what *ought* to be done, rather than on what *is* going on, which may be described as the *de*scriptive position.

It is in the nature of residential practice that staff are continually presented with situations that require immediate resolution. It may be that an old person has fallen down, or that there are complaints about a resident wandering into someone else's room and picking things up, or that an argument has broken out between two residents which needs rapid arbitration, or that someone wants permission to do something, and so on. Whether the incident itself is serious or trivial, there is a continual demand for on-the-spot decisions and action, without very much time for reflection if the potentially disruptive effects of the incident are to be contained and the establishment restored to an even keel. Clearly, the appropriate skill to deal with such a situation is to be able to make rapid judgements –

often on the basis of fairly scanty information – and to apply them with every appearance of conviction. There are no prizes in residential practice for dithering, or for reflection on the long-term consequences of one's actions.

This situation contrasts with that in field work, which may explain why good field work practitioners are not necessarily good residential workers and vice versa, and to a certain extent accounts for the tension that often exists between the two sides of the profession. In residential practice the decisions made and the sanctions governing the lives of the residents are generally – although not always – fairly trivial. They do not appear, at any rate, to have long-term consequences, although a number of them repeated over time may do so. They are merely nudges to correct deviations from the expected course of the life of the establishment. In field work, on the other hand, the social worker is not present with the client for the majority of the time, and beyond counselling and emotional support, the decisions that are made (almost always after consultation with seniors) are fairly crude but powerful. Moreover, they may well involve committing the department to the use of some of its resources in a way that is not involved when someone is already in residential provision. The field worker can receive a child into care, arrange for home-help services, act as advocate with official bodies, and so on. Decisions to act in such a way do not have to be made on the spot, and indeed are often too serious for that; so the field worker develops a much more descriptive outlook, in which she concentrates on discovering all the circumstances of the case, and speculates about the likely outcome of any given course of action before committing herself to it. Pearson (1975) concludes rather unkindly that field workers are 'professional ditherers' – but one can see his point.

The difference between the styles can be seen clearly when one gets a mixed group of field and residential social workers discussing a case. While the tendency is for the field workers continually to seek more information without wishing to commit themselves to any courses of action other than those of consultation with others, the residential workers tend to jump in much earlier with concrete proposals: 'Have you thought of . . .?', 'Why don't you . . .?'.

It is clear that both descriptive and prescriptive styles of thinking are valuable and necessary in their place, but both have their disadvantages in practical terms as well as theoretically. While the field worker's apparent woolliness does little to reassure the anxious client, the residential worker dispenses fairly rough justice, often according to a code of shame-culture rather than guilt-culture (Benedict 1967). She may be seen as insensitive, and because of the pressures to act, may fall back on her own particular 'recipes' – standard courses of action that are applied to a variety of superficially similar situations, often expressed as 'Whenever such-and-such happens, I always . . .'. This leads to a lack of flexibility, and ultimately to treating the residents as if they were less than fully human. The reference point for such recipes is invariably the idea of getting things to cool down for the establishment to run smoothly again.

HOMOEOSTASIS

The jargon word homoeostasis means 'balance' – specifically the balance between the internal world of a system and its environment. One of the reasons why we can think about residential establishments as if they were closed systems is simply that the overall dynamic of getting the establishment to run smoothly is one of homoeostasis, partly between the system as a whole and its environment, and partly between the parts of the system.

Homoeostasis is best illustrated in the first instance by reference to a biological analogy. Warm-blooded animals are much more flexible in their responses to the environment than cold-blooded animals, because of their capacity to maintain a stable internal environment almost regardless of the temperature outside. If the weather is cold, cold-blooded animals like reptiles become sluggish and unable to respond quickly to situations of threat, for example. Snakes and lizards have to spend hours basking in the sun to soak up enough energy to go about their daily business. Warm-blooded animals on the other hand have internal temperature control mechanisms that enable them to behave in roughly the same way whether it is warm or cold. When the weather is cold they burn up fat in order to keep warm; when it is hot they sweat or pant to cool down. This constant internal activity to keep the inside of the system steady in relation to the external changes is homoeostasis. Similar mechanisms lead to human experiences of being hungry or thirsty and being satisfied, as well as contributing to much more complex bits of social interaction.

Homoeostasis only works within certain defined limits, however. While the cold-blooded creature goes into a state of virtual suspended animation when it gets too cold to do anything, there is no such option for its warm-blooded counterpart. If human beings get too cold for too long (particularly if they are old and their internal temperature control is not as good as it was) they suffer from hypothermia and die. If they get too hot for too long, they suffer dehydration and heatstroke and can die. While there are obvious evolutionary advantages in being able to cope with a wide range of environmental conditions, no animal has yet conquered them completely – although human beings, whose response is to attempt to change the environment (switch on the central heating) are better at it than most.

Homoeostasis can also work economically or otherwise. As I write this, I am in my study with the gas fire on and the window open. Clearly, the maintenance of a comfortable and stable internal environment in the study under these circumstances is going to require much more energy input than if I had the window closed, and even more than if the room were totally insulated. Some systems have to work very hard to maintain their steady state, whereas for others very little effort is required.

In the case of the residential establishment, homoeostasis naturally involves many transactions across the boundary of the system: food, fuel, power, staff, money, and of course residents have to be brought in, and rubbish, waste, staff who have done their work, and residents who no longer need the provision have to be disposed of in order that the internal world can remain relatively the same. If there are drastic changes in the external environment, there may have to be changes inside, too, to adjust. Staffing levels may have to be raised or lowered, resident numbers change, and so on. In the end one may reach a point at which one says that the establishment is not the same one as it was at some time in the past. It has the same name, and perhaps nominally the same task, and even occupies the same building, but staff and residents and perhaps most of all the internal culture have changed so much that it is no longer recognizable. That is equivalent to the death of something – probably of an image of the establishment held by the person who no longer recognizes it.

It may initially be difficult to recognize that the urgent cry, 'Better tidy up this office – the Director's paying us a visit today!' is part of the overall process of homoeostasis, but it is. This need for balance results in constant first-order change within the establishment, and given that most of the physical aspects (such as the control of the heating itself, and the ordering and cooking of food) are dealt with with little need for direct attention, most of this first-order change is at the social and primary client-care levels.

THE STAFF THERMOSTAT

Turning from the biological analogy to a simpler one – that of a central heating system – we can say that the role of the staff in the day-to-day running of a residential establishment is like that of a thermostat.

The function of a thermostat in a central heating system is to maintain a relatively constant temperature in the rooms concerned by the operation of a negative feedback loop. It senses the temperature in the room, and if it is below the pre-set limit on the thermostat, it switches the heating system on. The effect is that the temperature begins to rise. When it has reached the desired pre-set level, or perhaps a little above that, the thermostat switches the heating off. The temperature then begins to fall as heat seeps away through the walls and the people in the rooms open and close doors, and when it has fallen far enough the thermostat cuts the heating back in again. And so it goes on.

All that the thermostat can do is to control, or govern, the system. It cannot create any of the energy to do the heating. If it is set at 20°C, but the outside temperature is freezing and the heating system cannot raise the internal level beyond 15°C, even going full blast, the most sophisticated thermostat is irrelevant.

The thermostat is effectively concerned with the creation and control of first-order change. It keeps things changing so that there is an appearance of no change. In fact, all it manages to do is to contain the fluctuations in temperature within a reasonable bound. If I set a domestic thermostat at 20°C, it may well not switch off until the temperature reaches 22°C and then allow it to drop to 18°C before it cuts in again. The average temperature will then be about 20°C. (This lag between the switch-off and the switch-on temperatures is called the *hysteresis* lag). In a finely tuned technical process, of course, this total of 4°C discrepancy may not be tolerated, and it may be necessary for the system to cut in and out far more frequently, so that the variation is 0.5°C or less. A representation of the variation of temperature over time is provided in Figure 3.1.

The activity of staff in a residential establishment is very like this. The variable being controlled is not the temperature – there may be a number of variables – but the effect is the same. For at least 80 per cent of the time in the case of junior staff, and perhaps a little less in the case of senior staff, their activity is directed to sensing predictable or unpredictable variations from the norm or reference standard, which they carry around in their heads, and intervening in the social system of the establishment to correct those variations and to make sure that the establishment stays within its defined limits, that is running smoothly.

Predictable variations from the norm are anticipated by most of the routines of the day. The residents will require meals, for

Figure 3.1 Influence of thermostatic control on temperature over time. (Second-order change is created by changing the temperature at which the thermostat is set.)

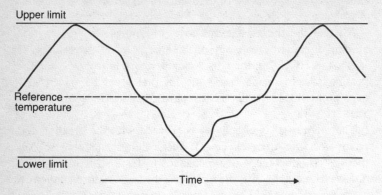

example, and possibly toileting or bathing. Unpredictable variations are minor crises that routinely occur: a dispute between residents, a resident who needs to be comforted, another who needs control.

In residential work with children and young people, the more appropriate analogy may be with the thermostat in a refrigerator. The natural tendency of the uncontrolled system seems to be for the social temperature to rise – for the kids to get too 'high' – and hence the function of the staff is to keep it down – to 'cool it'. Each staff member has in his head an idea of an acceptable level of activity and noise and deviance in a group of residents. When this is exceeded, he steps in to bring it down within limits again. Occasionally, he may feel that the social temperature is too low and too flat, and so he tries to get some activity going to liven things up. Although there is probably a consensus among the staff about the appropriate social temperature, many disputes that arise among them can be traced to slightly different assumptions as to when it is appropriate to intervene and when things can be left alone. The very active interventionist staff member will effectively have closer upper and lower limits, whereas his more 'laid-back' colleague will have looser ones, being able to tolerate more uncertainty. Which approach is 'better' is not at issue here, but it can be noted that the more value–committed establishments, whether their 'myths' (see Chapter 7) are punitive or therapeutic, tend to have closer limits than those with a more relaxed and pragmatic approach.

'Fixing' Residents

Creating stability in the establishment at large means keeping parts of the system the same, as far as possible. This means a tendency to 'fix' residents (and staff) in roles and not to acknowledge the possibility of change in them. Precedents are established for exercising the thermostat function, like the recipes mentioned earlier, and it is always easier to apply these than to look carefully at the system as a whole and to decide afresh on each occasion how the situation should be responded to. Growth and development on the part of residents is not catered for:

At a hostel for people with a mental handicap, the morning was always a rushed time; residents had to get up, wash, dress and have breakfast before the bus came to take them to the Social Education Centre. It was known as a 'fact' that one woman who was also slightly disabled physically was unable to do up her buttons, and so it was standard practice for staff to help her. Eventually she learned to do them for herself, with much effort and concentration, and was very proud of this. Unfortunately it took too long – sometimes up to a quarter of an hour for a 15-second job, and so staff would do them for her. Naturally after a while she did not bother. She probably felt put down by staff not letting her do things for herself, and certainly did not acquire any further new skills for a long time.

A lady in an old people's home suffered from arthritis, but it was the policy to keep residents as ambulant as possible for as long as possible, and so she made her way to the dining room with her frame at each meal time. It was not until she had taken to setting off from the lounge a full hour before the meal so that she could sit down for a rest in the toilets half-way down the corridor, and then there had been several occasions on which her absence from the dining room had been noticed and she had been found crying clinging to the hand-rails in the corridor, that it was finally acknowledged that she could have a wheelchair.

In a hostel for people recovering from a mental illness, where the declared philosophy was therapeutic and rehabilitative, all activities were reviewed in group meetings. When asked about how a boat trip on the river had gone, for example, the residents would either be non-committal or say they had enjoyed it and recount some anecdotes from it. Such contributions produced little reaction from the staff, but when one member volunteered how anxious he had felt on stepping onto the boat, the staff pounced and encouraged him to talk at length about his fears. Other residents then joined in in the same vein, and the discussion was subsequently held to have been a good one. In their concern to be therapeutic, however, the staff could well have been reinforcing the residents for expressing their weaknesses and inadequacies, rather than building up their competence and abilities, ready to survive in the outside world.

In each example, the norm was different. In the first one, it was based on the administrative convenience of keeping to a timetable; in the second to a committed value-position of keeping residents mobile; and in the third to an explicitly therapeutic aim. In each case, however, inability to recognize or promote change in the capabilities of the resident in question (whether for the better or for the worse) led to a disservice. The smooth running of the establishment was defined in terms of adherence to the norm.

DISCOVERING THE NORM

It is just possible to conceive of a system in which each new member of staff is given a rule-book that specifies clearly what the acceptable levels of conduct are for the residents, and what constitutes a violation ('All residents must have a bath at least twice a week'; 'All residents must be ready for the bus by

8.50 a.m.'; 'All residents are deemed to be capable of walking unless demonstrated otherwise by at least three recorded instances of a fall not precipitated by external acts'; and so on). To a certain extent prisons are like this, and all establishments must have some set rules and procedures. But such rules cannot cover every possible eventuality. Even if they could, they would have to be interpreted, and the question of the norm that they embody is only pushed one stage further back to that of the nature of the norm in the mind of the writer of the rules. No, what happens in practice is that staff are rapidly socialized into having a general idea in the back of their minds as to what this norm is, and they interpret situations in the light of this idea, or *working myth*.

One of the big issues in residential practice is finding out what this myth is, in any given establishment. It embodies certain assumptions about acceptable levels of comfort for the residents, acceptable levels of risk (these are often made more explicit than other aspects), acceptable levels of freedom, and so on. If, as I have suggested, about 80 per cent of the time of junior staff is spent detecting variations from this norm and correcting them, it is clearly the most important determinant of the form of practice in the establishment. It is not easy to spell out, because by its very nature it is inarticulate. How do you recognize the face of a friend? You would only be able to give me the vaguest approximation in words, but your accuracy in recognizing that face in practice is formidable. That is tacit (unspoken and unspeakable) knowledge, and the working myth of a residential establishment is at a similar level. In the chapters that follow I shall try to disentangle some more of the strands that go to make it up.

4 Hierarchy of Concerns in Residential Establishments

The previous chapter examined the way in which residential establishments seek to keep running smoothly – but left aside the *level* at which they function. One of the most difficult tasks for anyone trying to evaluate the performance of residential provision is to determine what can reasonably be expected, particularly when residential settings can take so many different forms. In this chapter I try to set out not a set of criteria for the direct assessment of performance, but a general model to guide discussion of the level of an establishment's practice.

MODELS AND PRIORITIES

A model is a simplified picture of reality, and because it is simplified it can only illustrate at one time one or two features of the complexity of the real world. Without going into the arcane reaches of mathematical modelling, a major problem for anyone who tries to design a model for others to use is whether the model reflects the *priorities* of the real world as they are understood by those who have to live in it.

In teaching courses on supervision, I sometimes find myself going into some detail about the desirability of scheduling sessions at certain intervals, depending on the needs of the staff member, and about the ideal setting for the conduct of supervision – only to be interrupted by the cry 'That's all very well, but how do we find the time to do it at all?'

A unit for adolescent girls had a psychoanalyst as an external consultant. He conducted very interesting sessions with the staff group about the deepest needs of the girls, but the staff did not learn anything because their major concern was how to get the girls to go to bed before the morning, and the complaints from the neighbours about roller-skating around the streets at 3 a.m.

MASLOW'S HIERARCHY MODEL

It is precisely its ability to deal with the question of priorities that accounts for the popularity of one of the best-known models in humanistic psychology – Maslow's 'Hierarchy of Human Needs' (Maslow 1987). (Fig. 4.1) It can be arranged as a staircase with five steps (although sometimes it is depicted as a pyramid – which is the same as looking at the staircase from the bottom instead of from the side).

Figure 4.1 Maslow's Hierarchy of Human Needs

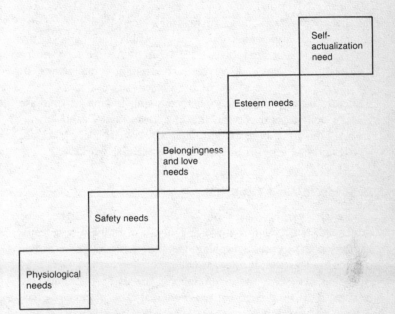

The basic principle of the model – which is *de*scriptive and not *pre*scriptive in intention – is that it is not possible to proceed to a higher step on the staircase until one has *adequately* satisfied the needs of the present step (and hence all preceding steps). It is not necessary to satisfy them completely (since this is not possible), just adequately. Maslow maintains that much confusion in psychological, ethical, and political debate stems from a failure to understand the steps with which the protagonists are concerned.

In order to be bothered at all about safety needs, it is necessary that physiological needs be reasonably satisfied. Physiological needs can never be completely met; they include hunger and thirst, for example, and however well I ate last night, I shall still be hungry again by lunch-time today. If there is no other way of doing it, I would be prepared to risk all kinds of danger, injury, and possibly death in order to meet those physiological needs; only when I have some assurance about the next meal arriving, albeit at some risk, can I become concerned about my safety and even comfort – as an individual. Assured of that to an extent that satisfies me, I can then start to pay attention to companionship, but probably not unless my physiological and safety needs are assured. And so I go up the ladder to the final state of self-actualization – the nature of which is beyond the scope of the present discussion.

Before moving on to see whether a similar kind of staircase can be built to describe the life of a residential establishment, three points emerge from the Maslow model that are particularly worthy of attention by residential workers.

Individuality and Community

There are various bases on which Maslow's model can be criticized, but a major one is the individualism that pervades it. Consider the person climbing the staircase not as a single person, but as the devoted provider for her family. Generally speaking, the 'love and belongingness' needs do not come into play until the third step; but we know that is not necessarily true when we are thinking about close family relations – and particularly the paradigm case of the provision of a mother for her child. In many respects, they can be considered one person – if the physiological needs of the child are not being met, the mother (and possibly the father) is not likely to exhibit concern for personal safety needs. When using this model to assess the level of human functioning one should also take into account the extent of family commitment as an independent variable. This does not invalidate the model as a whole, however, because it may be taken as starting from the position of the individual alone in an inhospitable world, and the renunciation discussed below comes into play at a later stage.

Renunciation

Given the opportunity for consistently adequate satisfaction of needs, it is possible for people self-consciously and deliberately to renounce the satisfaction of more basic needs in the interests of those of a higher order. Thus there are people who are prepared to put themselves at risk in order to save their companions, or to renounce belongingness in order to seek self-actualization in isolation from others. Lower-order needs may therefore be sacrificed, but only when the individual has to hand the potential for their fulfilment. Otherwise he is giving up nothing. The starving man is not the same as a man on a fast. The lonely man who says people are no good is not the same as the hermit; the former is a case of sour grapes, a rationalization for one's own lack, the latter is consciously renouncing what is potentially available.

These two cases need careful distinction in the case of clients. The issue probably shows most dramatically in the cases of children who come into care, and of some old people. The case of the child who exposes himself to risk — 'excitement' in his terms — because he has had a life without risk is quite different from the child who has never known anything else but risk. The former may commit offences 'for the hell of it', and need something that will offer him more 'constructive' risks to take; the latter commits offences because he finds life so precarious that he cannot afford to consider such niceties as the law when deciding how to act. The isolated old lady who reluctantly comes into an old people's home may be isolated as an act of conscious withdrawal, in which case it is important to respect her privacy and not to draw her into socializing when she does not want to. Or she may simply be abandoned and lonely because her friends have died and her family has moved away and life has become a struggle in which bothering to maintain contact with others has become very low on her list of priorities; in which case she may welcome opportunities to be sociable. Her situation may of course be a combination of the two, but in any case sensitivity and flexibility are required rather than the automatic assumption that 'she is that way because she wants to be' or 'we've got to bring her out of herself'.

Getting Stuck

Probably the most common point on the staircase for users of residential provision to have reached, and for them to be stuck at, is the transition from 'belongingness' to 'self-esteem' needs. If I am really hungry for the company of others, I will accept it on any terms – just as long as I can *belong*. I will be the scapegoat, the fall-guy, the butt of all the jokes, the whore – it does not matter how debasing the role, as long as others notice me, perhaps need me a little, and let me belong. Children in care and people with a mental handicap trying to carve out a place for themselves in what the jargon calls 'the community' are particularly likely to be stuck at this level – and it is often reflected in their relations with the staff of the establishment in which they live. Getting angry disciplinary attention from staff is better than no attention. In the language of Transactional Analysis, 'negative strokes are better than no strokes'. It is possible to get so stuck at this level that one dare not strike out for the next (self-esteem), in case one loses everything. Self-esteem is at least in part *being prepared to belong as long as it is on one's own terms*. One can only insist on one's own terms if the belonging can in some measure be taken for granted. I know other people need me for the football team, because it's my ball – so I'm not going to play unless I can be a striker. I already know lots of people and I am accepted and liked by them, so I do not have to stand here and suffer snide remarks and jokes at my expense: that is self-esteem. Many clients (as well as many other people who never become clients) find it a terrible risk to attempt to move on from the belongingness level; and after a few years (or even a few weeks) of learning that being accepted by others is not automatic but conditional, many such people do not know how to accept a positive view of themselves at all. The only attention they can relate to is critical, unpleasant, 'put-down' attention, particularly from those in some kind of authority. They discount compliments, reassurance, and support. They abuse trust, some may mutilate themselves, they encourage negative labelling, and yet in other situations when others may be dependent on *them*, they prove to be reliable, competent, and caring. Such inconsistencies and anomalies make sense if one accepts that some people are stuck at belongingness needs.

THE RESIDENTIAL STAIRCASE

The Maslow staircase is very generalized and designed to apply to all people at all times. A similar model of priorities for a residential establishment is paradoxically more complicated to devise because it is more limited in scope, and therefore has to do justice to the peculiarities of the residential setting as well as to those features that it shares with other situations. The point has also already been made that no one has a total view of what goes on in a residential establishment. This absence of a single perspective means that it is not really possible to speak of the 'needs' of such a system. The needs from the point of view of the residents may not be the same as those seen by the staff, which may in turn differ from the needs identified by the management of the agency. It is, however, possible to devise a staircase based on what I have called 'concerns'. These concerns are not merely feelings, however; they can be expressed in quite concrete terms.

If we start from the basis that the major input into the system (*i.e.* the service delivery system) of a residential establishment is the work of the staff, and that this can be assessed in terms of time, then we can use *staff time* as the major variable governing what can be done in a given establishment. We can substitute 'that which occupies staff time', or more elegantly 'concerns', for the notion of 'needs' used by Maslow. The actual steps on the staircase are deduced from an analysis of the systemic priorities in the residential task itself, which means the consensus of expectations as to what may be achieved, and what is logically required by each step (Fig. 4.2).

Figure 4.2   Hierarchy of concerns in residential establishments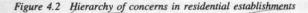

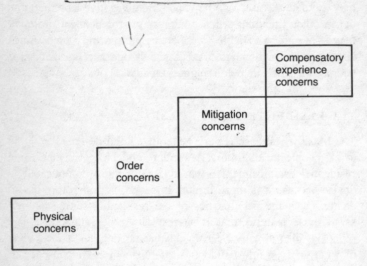

Physical Provision

We may begin with physical provision, since in the eyes of practically everyone that is basic to having a residential establishment at all. I have avoided the term 'care' because it carried too many connotations of dependence. It is in the nature of residential establishments that they provide for the physical needs of residents, but 'caring' is very broad and suggests that people are unable to do things for themselves, which is not universal even among those who live in residential settings.

It is reasonable to expect that residents will be sheltered (from the elements), fed, and perhaps clothed by the establishment. There may be disagreement about the level of this provision, but the consensus is that it should be provided above a certain level. Note that the level may vary – in the workhouse system it was deliberately kept very low in order to discourage people from entering unless there was absolutely no alternative.

Physical provision may also extend beyond these common human needs when clients require it; it may include assistance with bathing, toileting, general mobility, and any aspect of day-to-day life where a resident's capacity to do things for himself is physically or mentally impaired. In the expectation of the general public as well as of those more directly concerned, physical provision also embraces safety. Since clients are frequently admitted to care for reasons of safety, it is necessary to assume that the residential environment will itself be safe. So this first step embraces the first two steps of the Maslow hierarchy, looking at the issues from an institutional rather than an individual perspective.

As with the Maslow model, provision has to meet an adequate standard, defined as the point at which this level of need ceases to be a preoccupation for either staff or residents. More clearly than in the brief sketch I have given of the basics of the Maslow model, however, we can see on this staircase that excessive concern with physical provision can militate against effective performance on the later steps, if only because the total amount of staff time is limited. Physical provision can be used as a means of exercising control, for example; this is quite frequently found in hospitals, in which the nursing system is supposedly concerned only with the physical care of the patients. Since the rationale of the general hospital is concerned with the physical well-being of patients, appeal to this provides a basis on which to command their co-operation. They may be rendered as physically, psychologically, and socially dependent as is consistent with their treatment in order to ensure that they do not challenge the system. 'Now, Mr Jones' (to a patient who has been upsetting ward routine by going for walks around the hospital) 'don't you think you ought to be getting some rest? We don't want to tire ourselves out to soon, do we?' I leave aside physical means of manipulation, such as psychotropic drugs or even enemas, used to ease the task of control.

More commonly, however, too much concentration on

physical provision can impede the work to be done at the 'mitigation' level, which will be explored later.

Stuck at the Physical Provision Level

Regardless of the appropriateness of the level of physical provision, there are some establishments that remain stuck there, simply because there is so much to be done that there is no staff time left to devote to other levels. This situation characterizes a number of hospital units, both acute and long-stay. In acute wards, the absence of work at the higher levels may be of less importance, since stays are usually short and apart from their temporary physical disorder the patients are just as competent in the psychological and social spheres as anyone outside, allowing for the stress associated with being in hospital in the first place. On long-stay wards, however, the preoccupation with physical provision can be limiting. It shows most clearly on wards for severely handicapped patients and very old and frail people, where the sheer demands of performing physical tasks for the patients leave no time for anything else. If all the patients have to be spoon-fed, for example, feeding them is almost a continuous process – no sooner have the nurses finished giving them all their breakfasts, and toileted a few of them, then it is time to start again with lunch. No matter that studies have shown that many such patients can be helped to do much more for themselves than at present, there is just no staff time to put into operation the time-consuming stimulation and training programmes (Oswin 1971).

However grim that situation, it is at least easy to see how it might be improved, by increasing staffing levels. The tragedy is in those wards where the physical work is not so time consuming, but because the staff have no training or encouragement (or perhaps interest) to raise their sights beyond physical provision, they spend the remaining time sitting chatting to each other in the happy conviction that their work is done for the moment, while the patients sit or lie in blankness, becoming increasingly bored, disengaged, and disoriented (Townsend 1962). Alternatively they may fill any remaining time with increasing refinement of the physical provision, such as near-obsessive cleaning (Willcocks, Peace, and Kellaher 1987).

Order

Once a certain standard of physical provision has been reached and can be fairly predictably guaranteed, concern shifts to the matter of order or control within the establishment. 'Order' is my preferred term because it is broader than mere control, and does not carry the same connotations of gratuitous imposition on residents. Order may include control that is oppressive and persecutory, but not necessarily so.

It is of course perfectly possible to concentrate on order before physical provision, as a concentration camp might (let us not forget that concentration camps are residential establishments, too) but such a scenario is sufficiently bizarre to be ignored for present purposes. Generally speaking order emerges as a separate issue only when the residents concerned are sufficiently able-bodied not to require constant physical assistance, because order issues are raised by the 'wilfulness' of residents.

Order as a Distinguishing Feature

It is possible to argue that a self-conscious concern with order is what distinguishes a residential establishment from a hotel. Although it appears that the cheaper the tariff of a hotel the more rules there are likely to be, because staffing is lower and therefore all the variations of guests' preferences cannot be catered for, the general assumption within the hotel trade is that the guest or customer is a self-determining person who can do what he likes, and will not be considered a nuisance to other guests until proven otherwise. (Incidentally, this assumption does not always hold good for Youth Hostels, in my experience, even when the member is not a 'youth'! The working myth of youth hostels is an interesting conundrum; see Chapter 6.) In part this view of the guest stems from the fact that he is clearly a *customer* who is paying his own way. It would be interesting to research the views of staff about order issues in private residential Homes for elderly people where residents pay fees out of their own pockets (or, if paid for by the state, have at least the theoretical option of taking their custom elsewhere), and in hotels where the guests receive bed and breakfast and the costs are met under the provision for homeless persons.

Certainly it appears that in social work-oriented establishments, there is a general assumption that it is permissible, desirable, and even necessary to interfere in the lives of the residents more than in a hotel. Without some justification for doing so, staff are likely to feel at a loss, and that they are somehow not doing 'social work':

A student was placed in a girls' hostel run by a voluntary organisation. At that time – although not at other times in the history of the hostel – things were running very smoothly. Most of the girls were at work or in the latter stages of schooling or at college, and they got up and went to their respective day-time occupations as a matter of routine. In the late afternoon they would come in, have a meal, and then get ready to go out for the evening with their boy-friends, or stay in and study or watch television or play records, occasionally with visitors. The staffing ratio was low, and the staff on duty would spend most of their time in the office or chatting casually to the girls, or doing some domestic work in which the girls were not involved (although they did their own laundry and had a rota for cooking meals at weekends). The student was bored stiff, and felt very guilty because there was nothing for him to *do*. He was critical of the establishment and wanted to introduce more 'social work' – he suggested counselling sessions and activity groups and a more formal shared responsibility structure, for example. But it made little sense to see the hostel in 'social work' terms at all: it made more sense to see it simply in 'hotel and catering ' terms. All the order and control was internalized by the girls. They socialised new arrivals into what was expected of them, supported friends who had moved on, and made their feelings known to any member of the group who was rocking the boat.

Staff intervention was effectively irrelevant, and to force it on the girls would be to devalue their maturity and confidence.

(It could, of course, have been the case that the girls had underlying problems that were not being resolved, but the authority of the hostel staff to engage with such problems was far from clear.)

Such a hostel is the exception rather than the rule among residential establishments, largely because if residents were all as competent as that group of girls, they would not be 'in care' in the first place. In most cases conscious ordering is only evident to the casual observer, or even to a member of the residential community, when it is seen as imposed or inappropriate. Ask the average TV viewer to comment on the editing of the last film he saw, and in most cases the question would be meaningless to him. Film editing is a prime example of the 'art that conceals art'. In most cases one only notices it when it is done badly, or perhaps when it is done dramatically to make a special point (as in the work of Eisenstein or Hitchcock). The same goes for order in residential establishments.

Order includes the organization of the routines, the necessary interventions to enable residents to live together in considerable intimacy when they really share very little except someone else's view of their broad category of need, and the disciplinary activity of staff. However, it is a closed-system concept. As generally practised, it is a means of making sure that relations within the establishment itself are fairly smooth. From the viewpoint of order, it does not matter whether the patterns of conduct developed by residents would help or hinder them in living in the outside world – that is a refinement that has to wait until it can be afforded.

Explicit and Implicit Order

In some establishments, order is a big issue. If one has a unit full of people who do not want to be there – as in many establishments for young people or for offenders and in some others as well – it is easy to see that it can take up most of the available staff time after the physical aspects of the provision have been dealt with (and the physical concerns in such establishments are often seen as the province of the domestic staff anyway). If one is afraid of 'what might happen' every time one goes on duty, then it is only to be expected that there will be little energy to spare for other issues. As with physical provision, it is not possible to move on to the next step until order is sufficiently taken for granted not to be a problem. This may be achieved through the internal order exercised by the residents or through the assurance of adequate structures to deal with any problems that may arise, whether those structures be the convening of a community meeting or the use of draconian sanctions.

My own experience suggests that more establishments are stuck on the order step than anywhere else, just as more individuals are stuck on the 'belongingness' step than anywhere else. Even in old people's homes, where to the outsider there would seem to be few order issues to bother the staff, it remains a preoccupation. Staff have to overcome a basic fear of chaos, of what would happen if order were lost, and it only takes one or two incidents in which that fear is justified to make it loom large in staff perceptions even after the threat has faded away into nothingness. It takes both an act of faith and a positive vision of what lies beyond order to enable staff to move on, and neither is easy. There are too many establishments in which the vision of the staff is limited, and they cannot see what lies beyond order; in that case all that they can do with any time left over from asserting it at a basic level is to seek to make it ever tighter. These are the places that become oppressive and totalitarian and give a bad name to residential work.

Mitigation

Order is a closed-system issue. That is to say, the focus of attention is on the behaviour of the residents within the walls and grounds of the establishment. In order to internalize order, they have to learn to adjust to life within the unit, and external controls are used to make that possible. It does not matter that life in residential provision is 'unnatural' or 'artificial', and that the skills required to share a living space with forty other people are quite unfamiliar and irrelevant to most people's lives 'outside'.

Such preoccupation with behaviour in the closed world of the establishment leads ultimately to institutionalization. But that is not the only problem associated with residential life. It is generally held that living in a residential setting is itself stigmatizing, and in the history of the individual there are inevitably outside problems that have led to admission to 'care' (Wagner 1988), and the admission itself is a crisis (see Chapter 9, and Brearley *et al.* 1980). Although many establishments, particularly those that do not regard themselves as providing permanent 'homes' for residents, see themselves as providing 'treatment' or 'training' in one sense or another, aspirations to do so cannot be met until problems of stigma, undue dependence, and artificiality have been overcome.

For these reasons, the next step on the staircase must be that of *mitigation*. To mitigate something is to diminish its negative effects, and logically this precedes any concern with benefits. Logic, however, is not the whole story. While discussion of physical provision and order was fairly straightforward, mitigation and compensatory experience are more complex.

First there is the assumption made by a number of practitioners that mitigation does not have to precede compensatory experience. They have very sophisticated treatment regimes that offer a highly specialized experience to the individual, and maintain that these are sufficiently therapeutic to overcome the adverse effects of taking place in a setting different from that of the everyday world of most people. They may even deny that being in residential provision *has* any such adverse effects – that any problems experienced are imported from previous experience outside and that in a well-run establishment they are irrelevant. Such a view is likely to be taken by some at least of the therapeutic communities.

Issues in Crossing Boundaries
However, even staff working in therapeutic communities are

concerned about the problems of making the transition from that world to the outside, where the rules are very different. The language in which feelings are expressed and behaviour described is not the same inside as outside. Outside, there are no rewards for confrontation of every bit of behaviour that may be deviant or symptomatic of an underlying problem; even in the bluntest and frankest cultures there is some premium on tact and getting along with other people. Nor may disabling problems be greeted outside the residential community with understanding any expectations appropriate to the individual's capabilities; if you cannot do the job as well as anyone else, you tend to be out on your ear. If you do not pay the rent, the landlord is not interested in deep-seated personal reasons. The dominant ideology of the 'outside world' is not therapeutic concern, but *evaluative behaviourism* – people look simply at your behaviour and label it according to its impression on them, as 'lazy' or 'stupid' or 'irresponsible'. Problems associated with those different values are likely to account for more 'breakdowns' than the simple resurgence of a personality problem. More than that, coping with the stigma associated with having been 'inside' a prison or a psychiatric hospital, or having been in care as a child, demands more of a former resident than is ever asked of a 'normal' person.

Issues of mitigation in therapeutic communities can only be left out of account when the residents themselves deal with them without external assistance. In the case of short-term programmes concerned with very specific acute problems, it is quite possible for a resident to accept the specialized nature of the community for what it is, and to return to her previous perceptions and conduct in most areas of her life with only a momentary disorientation when she leaves. This, of course, may account for the relative ineffectiveness of the 'short, sharp, shock' regime for many young people who spend a matter of weeks in a detention centre. But once being in a specialized environment becomes a way of life, and perhaps even more if it is seen by the resident to be helping her, she gets out of step with the outside world, and may even be unable ever to make the transition back again.

So the sequence of steps on the staircase still holds even if the residents handle mitigation for themselves. It is then dealt with to an apparently satisfactory extent without taking up staff time, and can be ignored. But the sequence also holds if mitigation is ignored when it should not be, because then the compensatory experience is rendered invalid. Any empirical judgement about such considerations, of course, can only be made on the basis of follow-up research.

This is where the second issue about mitigation comes in. We are now moving outside the closed system of the establishment. Almost by definition, mitigation only makes sense when it is seen to apply across the boundaries of the establishment and in the outside world. It may be mitigation of a feeling of failure or guilt that has resulted in being admitted to residence in the first place; it may be mitigation of the effects of a trauma or crisis that caused the admission. It may be mitigation, as we have discussed, of the burden imposed by having to make the transition out of the establishment and back to the 'real world'. Whatever the case, it requires sensitivity to the outside as well as the inside on the part of the staff who attempt to handle it.

Mitigation and the 'Home'
This in turn raises the third issue. What about places that do become the residents' homes, which they do not expect to leave until they die? Do they, like some congregations of religious or the French Foreign Legion, regard everything that happened prior to entry as irrelevant and not to be mentioned? Or do they value the past life of the resident and try to help them to bring the good bits into the establishment as well as the bad? Many old people's homes encourage residents to bring as much furniture and as many personal effects and mementoes with them as practicable, and try to encourage continuing involvement with the younger generations of the family wherever possible. But once inside, does it matter that the way of life is so different from outside? Does the passivity of the lives of many elderly residents matter? Should they be 'allowed' or encouraged to retreat into their own memories and thoughts and not to engage with others any more than they seem at first sight to wish? Is

it mitigation to give such freedom, or is it mitigation to over-come the isolation of old age, to stimulate them and promote social interaction, and to learn new things? Ultimately that is a value judgement, but I can already hear the reader muttering, 'It depends on the person!'.

Indeed it does depend on the individual, and that is where the fourth complication of mitigation (and of compensatory experience) comes in. While physical provision applies to prac-tically everyone in the same way (with the exception of special diets and the like), and order subjects practically everyone to the same rules – although it may be more of an issue with some recalcitrant or cantankerous residents than with others – such a corporate view is not possible with mitigation. Everyone's problems in this area are different. Different because the factors leading up to admission were different, because the problems facing them on discharge will be different, because reactions to being in the establishment are different. There are of course common considerations, such as the acquisition of certain survival skills for young people or people with a handicap leav-ing 'care', but any programme that takes mitigation seriously has to move on from a generalized group view of the resident population to a much more individual one.

Practical Expression
So far the discussion of mitigation has been fairly abstract, but it does come down to very concrete issues, although the answers to the questions posed are by no means easy to deter-mine or sometimes to carry out once determined. Some of the simpler issues can be illustrated by reference to an establish-ment that seemed to have to got it all wrong:

In the early 1970s, when most local authorities had a considerable number of community homes for children, some of those belonging to authorities in large cities were situated outside the conurbations, which made visiting by families difficult, and hence impeded the rehabilitation of children back home. One authority had the idea of setting up an establishment within an area from which a substantial number of children came into care, specifically to receive children from the out-lying homes and to prepare them to return to their families. The problem was that the home was like a five-star hotel on the fringes of a very run-down inner-city neighbourhood. In 1972, when colour TVs were rare, the home had one. There were eight children in residence, with six staff and four domestic staff. The home achieved one of its objectives of getting the parents involved, but they – quite understandably – saw the quality of physical care their children were receiving, and had little or no interest in taking them home permanently. On Satur-day nights, the lounge was full of fathers and their friends watching 'Match of the Day' on the colour TV – but children only went home as the result of considerable pressure from field workers in the Department.

This illustration, slightly bizarre though it is, shows some of the problems of mitigation. Just as too high a level of order within the establishment can make mitigation difficult, so too can too high a standard even of physical provision. And yet, since physical provision is the first step on the staircase, it cannot be lowered very far in the interests of mitigation, which is only the third step. This dilemma also shows in other ways.

In 'independence training' units – and in fostering arrangements for young people over the school leaving age – many authorities have carefully worked-out policies governing deductions for lodging expenses from earnings or benefits. In many cases these require that amounts be set aside for lodgings, for food, and for clothing; but they ensure that *at least* a set amount remains for the young person's pocket money. Although the young people often resent making any contribution at all from what they see as their own money, nevertheless such policies still leave them in a fool's paradise compared with their situation when they leave care. Then, the cost of rent, heating and lighting, food and clothing will come first out of their income, and if they have any left at all 'for themselves' they will be lucky. Such a realization comes as a nasty shock on top of all the other traumas of leaving the protection of care.

There are other very practical expressions of the difficulties of mitigation. 'Ordinary life' or 'normalization' (hardly an 'ordinary life' word!) is now the watchword in the development of residential provision in many areas, but it tends to fall down when it conflicts with administrative convenience in the organization of the establishment. In ordinary life, people run out of things like milk or bread, and have to go out to the shops to get some. That does not happen in residential establishments. It seems like a very small thing, and indeed it is, but it leads to failure to anticipate such possibilities when living on one's own, and all adds to the stress of rehabilitation. Particularly in times of inflation, former prisoners returning to society find that they have not got a clue as to how much things cost; the same goes for residents who have never had to budget or buy essential items. Training programmes go some of the way to overcome these problems, but they can only offer simulations. Even if one were able to do the unit's shopping in the local supermarket instead of ordering over the telephone and signing the delivery note, buying for even eight or a dozen people (when a cook will actually prepare the food, and domestics will use industrial equipment to clean the house) bears little resemblance to buying for one or two with a very limited income, limited equipment, and limited skill.

Mitigating the Regime

Mitigation goes further than simple socialization into ordinary life. It must also pay attention to the extra pressures put on an individual by membership of a residential establishment. It is less easy to visit others and have visitors in a 'home'; it is less easy to find privacy (Parker 1988; Willcocks, Peace, and Kellaher 1987). It is almost impossible to make mistakes or take risks with real consequences and learn from them. The very address of the establishment can carry a stigma to those who know. One adolescent girl in care – who was certainly not unique – would get off the bus from school a stop too early and add another half-mile walk to her already considerable journey home lest any of her school friends discover that she lived in a community home. And what about residents who wish to spend a night at a friend's house and find that it has to be 'vetted' by a social worker before they can go? It is an understandable procedure, undertaken with the best intentions, but socially profoundly handicapping.

At a deeper level still, there are the problems raised for the resident by the establishment's messages about him (see Chapter 2). Mitigating these messages is not merely a matter of adding something on to what is already done in the establishment, or spending more personal time with a resident, but also of scrapping some procedures or doing them differently to give different messages – and thereby once again calling into question the levels of physical provision and order already achieved.

Compensatory Experience

So to the highest step on the staircase. 'Compensatory experience' is the phrase coined to represent this one; I have tried to avoid the terminology of 'therapy' or 'treatment' or 'training' because of all the additional philosophical and technical issues they raise. This step is about the active provision of opportunities to have experiences that will compensate for the problems that brought the person into residential provision in the first place. In other words, if mitigation is concerned to ensure that a person's life is no *worse* for coming into residence, compensatory experience is designed to make sure that it is actively *better*.

This step is not appropriate to all residential establishments. There are those – such as some elderly people's homes – that are simply homes. Not only is it not clear what compensatory experience would look like for them, it is also doubtful whether they have authority from anyone to provide it. If someone has chosen to enter a residential establishment in order to be looked after when they are not able or willing to carry on looking after themselves, then not having the concerns of daily survival on their minds may free them to interest themselves in other things, but that is not an active intervention by the establishment in the course of their lives. The role of the institution is to provide a maintenance function, and that is all.

There are also some establishments where the precipitating problem that led to admission is not amenable to very much social assistance. This may be the case in an establishment for people with physical handicaps; the unit may take responsibility for ensuring that residents receive appropriate medical or physiotherapeutic help when required, and will provide such aids as may be needed to preserve mobility and capability as much as possible – but in the final analysis there is not much which can be done by the staff themselves to improve the residents' physical condition. On the other hand, there are circumstances where a great deal can be done, in helping people to cope with their handicaps in such a way as to be able to move out into the community again, either living in their own home once more, or being able to hold down a new kind of job (or even the same kind of job) while continuing to be a resident.

The difficulty is that compensatory experience is even more of an individual matter than mitigation. Every person's problem is different and needs a different approach, so it is unlikely that there are any establishments that are completely excused the need to provide compensatory experience for some of their residents.

Compensatory experience covers an enormous range of work. In some cases it is obvious. Adolescent units may specialize in independence training. Hostels for people with a mental handicap may also be preparing them for independent living in quite a different way. Establishments working with mentally ill residents may be engaged in quite intense psychotherapy, or work on specific issues like alcohol or drug abuse. Children's establishments may have an educational as well as a therapeutic task, or be working towards fostering placements. Old people's homes may be assisting their residents to overcome loss, to find new ways of enjoying their latter years, and preparing them for the last great adventure – death. Perhaps that example is not quite so obvious, but that only goes to show that work on this front is more varied than might at first be thought.

Some compensatory experience is more subtle. It may come from finding a role within the resident group that leads a person to discover new talents. It may come about as a sort of reverse of the problems that have to be mitigated; by no longer being a burden on a carer in the community or on a wider family group, a resident may find improved relations and respect within that relationship. It may be the change in outlook of a resident who felt her misfortunes were unique, and now discovers that she is not alone, and learns to transcend self-pity. The variations are endless, and in some cases the staff do not even know what they are doing.

They may even dismiss one of the most important contributions they make to the lives of residents. It is not uncommon for child care practitioners to complain, 'All we're doing is containing the kids – we're not doing anything with them!' The reality of this needs to be checked out, but it undervalues the very important work of containment. For many adolescents, their most important task is to grow up, and they may need to be 'held' so that they do not increase their problems while they are getting on with that job. To offer such containment is a vital form of compensatory experience, often not recognized or valued by anyone in the system – young person, residential worker, field worker, management, or parents.

That suggests that staff intentions are often not the best guide to what form of compensatory experience is being offered. But if that is so, how appropriate is it to see compensatory experience as the final step on the staircase? Is it not just something that happens, and if it does we applaud it but if it does not then we just sigh and throw up our hands? There are two factors that suggest this is not an adequate response.

First, staff time – as suggested earlier, this is the important factor in relation to all deliberate efforts to progress up the staircase. At the beginning of this section I was careful to refer to 'the active provision of opportunities to have experiences that will compensate for the problems . . .'. We cannot *provide* experiences for anyone. Only they can have the actual experiences for themselves. All we can do is provide the *opportunities* to have the experiences. Experiences are delicate plants, however. They need to be recognized and nurtured if they are to grow and bear fruit, and it is this task of encouragement that is central to the staff contribution, whether it be through planned interventions like counselling or group-work, or through almost spontaneous exploitation of the moment in the hour-by-hour work with the resident. If staff are preoccupied with other things, they will not be able either to do the group-work or counselling effectively (if at all), or to pay attention to the subtleties of communication that are the essence of that spontaneous work.

Preoccupation is the second issue – in this case the pre-occupation of residents. If they are worried about physical matters, about order, or about problems that may be mitigated, they will not be paying attention to the potential benefits of their situation. Such preoccupations will recur until residents are able to take for granted the more basic issues – and it should be recognized that this may take a long time, and some residents will never come to see that compensatory experience is a relevant concern of the establishment.

The Right to Offer Compensatory Experience

The residents' perspective raises an important ethical consideration – one that has been implicit in all the previous stages, including that of physical provision, but which shows most clearly here. By what authority do staff impose on residents their view of what a fulfilled life looks like, and get them to go along with it? This is the old question of values again. Even the kind of physical provision offered implies certain values, particularly in the way in which it is offered; they are sometimes referred to as 'middle-class' values. They are to do with having proper meals at set times, instead of grabbing a biscuit or bread and jam if you happen to be hungry. They are to do with sitting down to those meals at a table, instead of having it on your knee in front of the TV. They are to do with the desirability of regular baths, and not being smelly. and with having your own bedroom and even your own bed. Any of these may conflict with a resident's previous life-style, and the loss of similar trivial freedoms can mean a lot to some residents. But it is when someone who devises the programme of the establishment decides that some ways of life, even some ways of thinking about yourself, are *better* than others, that the real arrogance of social work shows through. There may be an almost perfect consensus among professionals in the field about the 'rightness' of what we are doing, but that should not blind us to the fact that we are nudging residents towards one set of values rather than another.

It is axiomatic that being educated is a Good Thing, that having a mature approach to problems (whatever that means) is a Good Thing, and so on. But compensatory experience designed to lead to the internalization of such values can even run counter to the mitigation process, because those values themselves may be at variance with those held by the community from which the resident hails (Curran 1972). Perhaps this shows most strongly in respect of residents who come from ethnic or cultural minority groups, but discrepancies show between the culture of the residential setting, and even mainstream groupings in our society. Social workers may believe strongly that women have equal rights; to adopt such a view and then to return with it to a community in which women's traditional roles are very circumscribed is to become isolated within that community, whether one is male or female, whether one is Moslem or a native North-Easterner.

It cannot be repeated too often that there is no alternative to taking up a position on such matters; not to do anything about them is as much a value position as to do something – but practitioners should at least be aware of what they are doing.

5 Of Sisyphus and Snowballs

One thing seems certain from the staircase model: all other things being equal (which they never are), it takes more effort to practise sophisticated residential social work then to operate a run-of-the-mill establishment. But what determines the level of practice for a run-of-the-mill establishment, and where does the energy come from for the extra effort? This chapter will attempt to present a model that goes some way towards answering those questions, and accounting for some of the issues surrounding change in residential work.

In Chapter 3 the idea of homoeostasis was introduced, and it was defined as a state of balance (more technically, 'dynamic equilibrium') between the internal world of the system and its environment. Such homoeostasis can never be static – it is necessary to work all the time at first-order change to achieve it. Nonetheless, systems 'find their own level', like water. They tend towards that state which requires least effort to keep it in being, and although homoeostasis requires perpetual work, it is nonetheless the state of least effort short of death.

However, the discussion left out of account the source of the values that determine the level of homoeostasis. The focus was simply on the amount of effort expended to keep things running smoothly. It is now time to expand the model a little, by suggesting the factors that go to make up the homoeostatic state.

ADMINISTRATIVE CONVENIENCE

Left to themselves, as it were, residential establishments settle at the level of administrative convenience. Administrative convenience is the practical expression of theoretical homoeostasis, in that it is the form of practice that requires least effort on the part of all concerned. It must be emphasized that even so, *practice at the level of administrative convenience requires a great deal of hard thought and work*. It may be the easi*est* option, but it is not easy.

It is not easy because administrative convenience attempts to satisfy all of the people all of the time. If a policy or procedure creates any unnecessary problems or hassle from any of the people who have an interest in the conduct of the establishment, it is by definition not administratively convenient. Such people are not only the residents and the staff, but the residents' relatives, the management of the agency, the political representatives who may control the agency, any watch-dog bodies that may oversee practice such as management committees, the financial controllers and auditors, and perhaps even the local press. That list will be recognizable to many senior practitioners, who are aware that their role is a balancing act between the often conflicting demands of the interested parties.

The standards of work at the level of administrative convenience are very variable, because they depend on the pressures exerted by the different parties. If one works for an agency that insists on certain high standards of practice and enforces them through constant monitoring, then the work produced is likely to be different from that in any agency that is basically profit-making and knows that it is in a seller's market, and therefore where the standards of provision are likely to be as low as one can get away with without falling foul of the press or the law. If the resident group and/or their relatives are vociferous and insistent on standards, and particularly if they put in the effort themselves to raise funds for the improvement of the service, the administratively convenient level is going to be higher than if the resident group is inarticulate and highly dependent, perhaps without outside support, and even afraid of the staff and management. In other words, power relationships have a great deal to do with the negotiation of the level of administrative convenience. In many cases, in the local authority as well as in voluntary and private sectors, a major source of power is holding the purse-strings, and the level of practice is constrained by the money available. In a similarly high proportion of cases, the voice of the residents is rarely heard, and when it is, it is easily ignored or silenced.

Whatever the absolute standard of provision under conditions of administrative convenience, the important characteristic is that it has no value base of its own, other than 'anything for as quiet a life as possible'. The practitioner at this level is perpetually trying to avoid battles, and if they cannot be avoided, to fight only those that are necessary to avoid greater ones.

In one old people's home, it was forbidden for residents to have ornaments, pictures, or other mementoes on dressing-tables or other furniture in their rooms. The residents accepted this as a matter of course, although they did not like it. The ruling had come about because the domestic staff had complained for some time that such obstacles impeded their efficient cleaning.

In another old people's home, care staff found it difficult to 'keep an eye on' some of the residents who were given to walking around the premises (or 'wandering', in the staff view), and in danger of falling. They adopted the expedient of removing some of the rubber webbing in the chairs in which these residents habitually sat, so that they sunk into the chairs and found it more difficult to get out.

In an establishment for adults with a mental handicap, breakfast was always beautifully laid out for the residents when they came down, even to the extent of the milk having been put on the cereals (which were of course invariably soggy by the time they were eaten). This was because milk was frequently spilt if the residents put it on themselves.

In these instances, poor practice was accepted by senior staff, or even instituted by them, in response to pressure from domestic or care staff who needed to find a solution to an inconvenience. External pressure to change was not adequate, because the senior staff had to live with the care staff all the time, whereas the Residential Services Officer or the equivalent was merely a nuisance who looked in occasionally, and in many cases never noticed the practices.

Practice originating from administrative convenience is not always poor, of course (although it is in the nature of things to find more examples where it is 'poor' than where it is 'good'):

It is not uncommon to find units where there are some interesting activities for residents, as a result of the enthusiasm of one or two members of staff. In some cases this is a committed harnessing of the talents of staff members with keen personal interests to the service of the overall task of the establishment; but in others there is little thought as to how the activity may be integrated with the task. It is simply added on because the staff have pestered for an opportunity to do something that they as individuals enjoy within working time. Outdoor pursuits are often developed in this way, as are football teams or craft activities.

In one community home with education, a gifted practitioner did some effective work with girls in the secure unit. However, the criterion for admission to the unit was that the girls had caused disruption in the rest of the establishment, and they were sent there to give the rest of the residents and staff a breather. The girls understood this pattern long before the staff latched on to it, and would create problems simply in order to be sent into the unit.

In a hostel for adults with a mental handicap, relations between residents and staff improved when care staff began to do the cooking at weekends, simply because of the difficulty of finding a cook for that period. However, this chore invariably fell to the lot of the female staff on duty, and they resented it; so as soon as a cook could be found, the previous pattern was re-established and staff and resident relations deteriorated again.

T.S. Eliot expressed it as 'The last temptation is the greatest treason/to do the right thing for the wrong reason.' The fact that something is not only good practice but is also administratively convenient does not totally invalidate it, but it should raise questions about its integration with the work of the establishment as a whole. In many cases it would take a lot more inconvenient effort to take full advantage of the opportunities offered.

One area in which administrative convenience really falls down, however, is illustrated in the second example above. The girls in the secure unit were 'playing the system', certainly, but by colluding with them for the sake of administrative convenience, the staff were really allowing them to develop their own 'treatment plans', in a way that was very different from a properly negotiated treatment contract. As not uncommonly happens, girls who caused trouble got more attention, and thus in behavioural terms got reinforcement for causing trouble – so they caused more trouble, and learned to do so. They also contributed to their own labelling, and to the notion that they could not be trusted. The very existence of the secure unit underlined that 'fact'. In other settings, there may be a premium on helplessness as a means of attention-seeking, rather than troublesomeness, or a combination of the two. In any event, the philosophy of administrative convenience, with its concern for short-term interventions to maintain homoeostasis, contributes to such 'anti-therapeutic' patterns.

ADMINISTRATIVE CONVENIENCE AND THE QUALITY OF PROVISION

In this business, easiest does not mean worst. As I have indicated, the quality of provision made or work done under conditions of administrative convenience is by no means necessarily poor. In fact, it would by definition require *more* effort to run a *worse* establishment that an administratively convenient one.

The way this works can be seen if we set up a notional graph, plotting quality of provision along the horizontal axis and amount of effort required along the vertical axis (Fig. 5.1). The graph can only be notional because it is of course not possible to quantify 'quality' (or 'effort') satisfactorily. There will even be disagreement about what constitutes 'quality', and how to recognize it when one finds it, but it is almost certain that arguments about quality centre around commitment to values; and the argument will hold whatever those values are, as long as one can also conceive of their opposites. In the examples, of course, I use my own value system, which is consistent with

Figure 5.1 Relation between effort and quality of provision

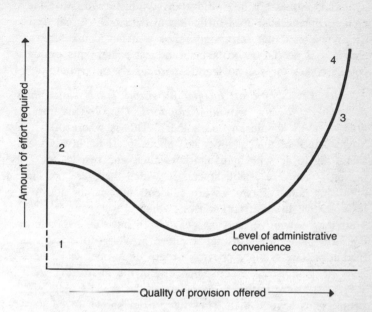

that of Wagner (1988). The basic message is that more effort is required in order to make both worse and better provision for residents than the standard of administrative convenience. Picking out the numbered features on the graph:

1. *The amount of effort needed to deliver any kind of residential provision is considerable.* The dashes on the vertical axis of the graph are a convention in graphics to represent the fact that the length of the line does not realistically indicate the factor it depicts. To repeat, even delivering residential services at the level of administrative convenience takes a very great deal of effort.

The sheer difficulty of doing the job at all is an important consideration in the shape of the curve. If the task were easy, it would naturally be expected that practitioners would express themselves and their values by adding extra touches to it, and would not take refuge in administrative convenience. But because it *is* difficult and demands a great deal of anyone, it is not surprising – nor is it any cause for shame – if people try to take the easiest route. This of course makes the second feature particularly interesting:

2. *It takes more effort to offer provision that is* worse *than the administratively convenient standard.* The obvious question is, 'Why should anyone bother?' This is where the broad values of the 'quality' axis come in. If quality is seen as having to do with humanitarian values and respect for persons, there are establishments in which these are not the dominant values. Examples are concentration camps and to a lesser extent the old workhouses, which are or were gratuitously punitive, and prisons, which have an overriding concern for security. Insofar as those in charge of these institutions are 'simply obeying orders' they operate at the level of administrative convenience. But the interesting and very sad feature is that in many cases the zeal of such people goes beyond that. They have been known to be so seduced by the power of their position as to put extra effort into the humiliation and oppression of their inmates. Once the inmate has been defined as a non-person, or as one who has somehow forfeited normal human rights, he or she can be victimized, exploited, tortured, and killed with every appearance of satisfaction by staff who put their heart and soul into their work.

In 1971 Zimbardo conducted the experiment of creating a simulated prison, in which half the volunteers were arbitrarily chosen as prisoners and half as gaolers. The experiment had to be prematurely ended after six days because of the behaviour of 'guards'and 'inmates'.

In less than a week the experience of imprisonment undid (temporarily) a lifetime of learning; human values were suspended, self-concepts were challenged and the ugliest, most base, pathological side of human nature surfaced. We were horrified because we saw some boys (guards) treat others as if they were despicable animals, taking pleasure in cruelty, while other boys (prisoners) became servile, dehumanized robots who thought only of escape, of their own individual survival and of their mounting hatred for the guards. (Zimbardo 1972).

The second question is, 'Why bother to include a reference to such obscene happenings in this discussion?' The answer is that unfortunately the situation is not wholly unknown within mainstream residential settings. There have been suggestions of such an attitude in the reports of inquiries into former approved schools and hospitals for mentally handicapped people and recent reports of abuses in homes for elderly people. This is the dark side of residential work, and it is probably better not to dwell on it, but the potential for such practice is there in any establishment, and no practitioner can afford to ignore it.

3. *It also takes more effort to offer provision that is better than the administratively convenient standard*. This is a much less contentious point, indeed an obvious one, but there is more to it than at first appears. If the level of administrative convenience is determined in part by the requirements of those in authority, then going beyond it will not necessarily command their support. Indeed, where the authority is suspect, it is often believed that if one does go beyond administrative convenience, that will be used as an excuse to cut resources or make greater demands on the establishment. However, since this is the position of major interest to us, we shall return to it in more detail at a later stage.

4. *There is a point at which increased effort does* not *lead to improved provision*. This is the other end of the scale from point 1. Again, it is unusual to encounter it in practice, but it is salutary to be reminded of it. All philosophies of residential service are flawed, and if carried too far they begin to defeat their own purposes. An emphasis on the

independence of residents ultimately leads to neglect. If shared responsibility is taken too far it becomes an abrogation of responsibility on the part of the staff; respect for privacy becomes a condemnation to loneliness; stimulation becomes nagging; care becomes smothering.

It can be seen that the curve in the 'graph' at first moves upwards very slowly, and then accelerates. This indicates that initially considerable improvements in the quality of provision can be made with little extra effort, but further along the curve, as it climbs ever more steeply, one can run oneself into the ground trying to do more and more, for less and less return. Indeed, it may be that the curve should really start to move backwards to the left, for two reasons: first because of the 'inherent contradictions within the system' identified above, and second because of the likelihood of burn-out on the part of the staff.

THE SOURCE OF EXTRA EFFORT

Returning to point 3 on the 'graph': the major question is where the energy comes from not only to make the extra effort initially, but to keep on making it. Some examples of administratively inconvenient practices may help to clarify the situation:

In a hostel for people with a mental handicap, there is a policy of encouraging – although not demanding – maximum involvement in the community, and on most evenings some residents are going out to visit friends from the Social Education Centre, to clubs or church activities, going swimming or roller-skating or to the cinema or just to the pub. This places severe demands on the staff. For some residents transport has to be arranged, for others an escort may be necessary or meals may have to be re-scheduled, there is a degree of anxiety about those who are out on their own, and those who stay in also have to be provided for.

An old people's home introduced a form of 'group living', although somewhat limited by the constraints of the building.

Small lounges and dining areas were created, and meals were carried to each group in heated trolleys. Apart from having to argue with the authority for the provision of the trolleys, staff also found that assistance to residents serving food out in small groups was very demanding, because there were no more staff available, but they had to go from one group to another. They also found that residents tended to argue more with each other about serving out, and their diplomacy was severely taxed.

What created these developments and enabled them to continue in existence was not the *knowledge* that it could be done, nor the *skills* to be able to do it. Both of these are important, and many innovations have collapsed because they have not been adequately researched and prepared for. But ultimately the important consideration was the *conviction that they were the right things to do*. Beyond a certain threshold, which is determined by factors such as staffing levels, the central question is, 'We may know it can be done, and we may know how to do it, *but is it worth the bother?*' The 'bother factor' can only be decided on the basis of the values of the staff group.

As in the previous chapter, the vision of the Head of Home (or whoever set up the idea) is a central factor, but the continuance of any working practice that requires extra effort rests on the acceptance of the extra effort or bother by the front-line staff themselves.

In the hostel for people with a mental handicap, the policy was undermined for several weeks after a honeymoon period by two long-serving members of staff for whom the routine of the evening and the supervision of the residents was more important than their community involvement. Each one would quietly find some reason why it was not possible to go out on this particular evening when she was on duty. This became apparent to other members of staff when it was their turn to do the evening duty and they found some residents sitting around as before, complaining that 'Mrs Brown said I couldn't go because . . .'. Given that the residents had initially had their own doubts about their capability to go out, persuading them that it was all right after all was more difficult than implementing the policy in the first place.

Winning over the staff group then becomes a central concern of senior staff, because experience makes it very clear that a shift of values will not be internalized simply as a result of management orders.

From Administrative Convenience to Working Myth

Once a set of values has been internalized by the staff group, it is only to be expected that they will wish to express them in practice. If those values have been fully internalized, the staff will find it difficult to work in any way that does not embody them. The effect of this is to shift the bottom of the curve of the 'graph' at least a little upwards and one hopes a little to the right (Fig. 5.2). The least effort option is no longer administrative convenience in the form in which it has previously been encountered. Instead it is a modified form that takes account of the power of the staff group in negotiations over what is administratively convenient, given that that staff group now holds a set of values that may be called the 'working myth'. (Working myths will be explored in greater detail in the next chapter).

Hitherto, the level of administrative convenience has been purely pragmatic. It has been based on what has kept happy significant parties within the system. Now one very significant party has raised the game somewhat by espousing a set of values, possibly at the instigation of the senior staff, but possibly as a result of influences from other sources. The values they espouse may be irrelevant to the quality of residential provision; they may for example (as happened in one school for 'maladjusted children') decide that it is very important to go to work looking very smart. This changes the pattern, in the sense that the previous level of effort is no longer enough, but in terms of the diagram it merely raises the curve a notch up the 'effort' axis. If the values are inimical to the quality of provision, they may be putting more effort into providing a service

Figure 5.2 The effect of internalized staff values

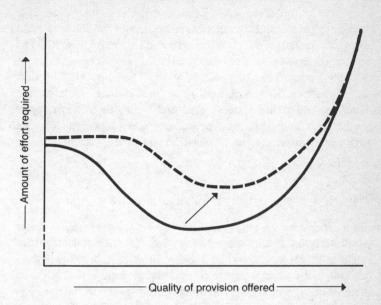

of lower standard to the residents. Some people claim that this was the case when residential workers went on strike a few years ago, although those involved counter by claiming that in the long term such action was in the interests of the residents. But say the staff decide, after a difficult period, that the residents are really an ungrateful bunch of so-and-so's who do not deserve all the attention they are getting – then the curve would move upwards (because a policy based on such a view would lead to conflict with management and external bodies) but to the left. (If the management and other bodies came to share the same viewpoint, the curve would settle down to its previous level on the vertical axis again, as long as the residents did not rebel.)

If, on the other hand, the staff group 'develops' in some way, attempting to improve the quality of their service, then the curve moves upwards and to the right.

Whatever the case, what has happened is the creation of a new level of administrative convenience, and the left and right ends of the curve still require more effort to implement. The major difference is that now, administrative convenience is based on some kind of value position. The same kind of shift might happen if another party in the system, such as the management of the agency, also had a change of heart, or if registration and inspection procedures were to be made more stringent (assuming no 'industrial deviance' to undermine them).

CHANGE – WELCOMED OR RESISTED?

The experience of many senior staff – and even more junior staff – trying to introduce change into a residential establishment is that it is like trying to roll a boulder uphill. It involves an enormous amount of effort, and the moment one lets up on that effort it begins to roll backwards again. If the push to change is neglected for a while, one finds that the boulder is back at the bottom of the hill and one has even less energy than before to start shoving again.

For several years, a generally 'good' community home had a problem with staff failing to write up the log. They would leave notes for each other, they would tell each other what had gone on at change-over meetings, and they would discuss incidents fully at staff meetings, but the entries in the daily log were either non-existent or perfunctory. This was commented on by visiting representatives of management from the Department, and by visiting councillors on rota visits. After such criticisms, the Officer-in-Charge would make a concerted effort to get the staff to change. He would inspect the log thoroughly whenever he was on duty, he would rebuke staff members who left scrappy bits of paper with notes for other staff instead of recording incidents properly, and he would raise the matter at staff meetings. For a few days or even weeks the log would be properly filled in, and the Officer-in-Charge would relax; and in a matter of days the situation would be exactly as before.

A similar situation obtained in an establishment for people with physical handicaps – this time concerning staff knocking on residents' doors before entering their rooms. The senior staff would have periodic purges on such issues, only to find that when they turned their attention to something else, staff reverted to their previous behaviour.

On the other hand, there are examples of situations in which similar changes have been welcomed with open arms by the staff group as a whole, and there has been no difficulty about getting them to stick. For some time I have been concerned with one particular innovation: the introduction of a programme of professional supervision, in a wide variety of establishments, for all client groups. In many cases it has been embraced enthusiastically, but in other superficially similar situations, it has been resisted and sometimes ultimately defeated. Since the staff acting as change agents had in every case been through a virtually identical training programme, and had returned with the same literature, and had had the same amount of management support, it is clear that the variation is not accounted for by the innovation itself. There remain several possibilities:

1. Some change agents (the people who came on the courses) were not really interested in introducing supervision. This is the *personal commitment* explanation.

2. Some attempts were blocked by suspicious members of the staff team. This is the *resistance* account.

3. Some establishments were just not ready for such a 'sophisticated' development. This is the *timing* account.

4. Some establishments were under too much pressure to spare the 'lead time' in which the supervision programme consumed more staff time and energy than it liberated. This is the *capacity* argument, and fits well with the hierarchy of concerns discussion in the previous chapter.

5. Some establishments found that supervision just did not fit in with their present established pattern of doing things. This is the *culture* reason.

Add to these the further possibility:

6. The lack of *commitment* of some of those attending the courses was a reflection of 3, 4, or 5, or possibly an anticipation of 2.

It becomes clear that the problem lies not so much in the innovation itself as in the *relationship between the innovation and the culture of the establishment*.

(I should add that in the majority of cases supervision was successfully introduced and to the best of my knowledge remained in effective operation, and that there were some cases in which I would agree that its introduction would not have been appropriate.)

I say 'the relationship between the innovation and the culture of the establishment' rather than referring solely to the culture of the establishment because that varied considerably. The 'successful' establishments included both those that were desperate for *something* to change an intolerable situation, and those that were running very well and were in search of a means of taking their development even further. But the same range was evident among the 'failures'. Examination of the innovation-culture system and the response of the culture may not necessarily enable one to get a particular innovation accepted, but it may reveal a great deal about the culture and therefore offer pointers to those innovations that may be accepted.

THE MYTH OF SISYPHUS

Sisyphus was a figure in the Greek underworld who was condemned forever to push a boulder up to the top of a hill. Whenever he reached the top, the boulder would roll down to the bottom again and he would have to start pushing all over again. Some writers, like Albert Camus (1975), have seen in this myth a paradigm of the whole human condition, but for present purposes we shall simply use it as a short-hand description of the kind of process that was examined above – a process that requires a continuous input of energy to keep it going (which is in fact true of all open systems).

Opposed to the Sisyphus situation is that rare, gratifying, and exhilarating experience when innovation is greeted with enthusiasm, and requires only the slightest push to start it rolling. As it rolls, it gathers momentum, and probably even size. More and more things are caught up in it, and it develops more and more energy of its own, to the extent that it may actually be difficult to stop. This is the Snowball effect.

The Snowball occurs when an innovation is recognized by the members of the community or staff team as moving in the direction of administrative convenience or the working myth, and the Sisyphus situation when it is seen as moving away from it. The 'recognition' component is important, because it is the way in which the change is *seen* by those involved that makes the differences, not the reality of the change (if there is such a thing).

There would seem to be two morals to this, but one of them is spurious. The first is the suggestion that one should confine oneself to changes that will become Snowballs, and avoid those that call for the labours of Sisyphus. That is all very well, but part of the problem is that we do not know which is going to be which until we have tried it. Not only that, but ease of adoption is far from the only criterion for the selection of a change; some of the changes that work like Snowballs may be seen as quite undesirable, and senior staff not infrequently find themselves in a sort of Sisyphus-in-reverse situation, in which they are standing on the slope trying to prevent the Snowball running over them and flattening them, and if possible halting its roll. The Snowball and Sisyphus sides of the valley of working myth are mirror-images of each other. The Sisyphus boulder on its way back down the hill becomes a Snowball, and trying to halt a Snowball rolling towards the valley is a labour of Sisyphus.

The second possibility is to examine what happens to any proposed change and to learn from it about the nature of the working myth in the establishment. Any Snowball change will contain factors, probably values of some kind, that are consistent with the working myth. Any Sisyphus change will contain elements that are inconsistent or dissonant with it. This is putting things the other way around – learning about the nature of the slope from the behaviour of the boulders, rather than assuming that one knows about the slope and can therefore select where to roll the boulders.

If this approach is pursued, then the investigator acquires another view of the culture of the establishment that may well change his or her priorities about change, in the direction of the creation of a different kind of working myth. In order to explore this further, it is necessary to go into more detail about the nature of the working myth(s) of a residential establishment, which is the topic of the next chapter.

6 The Working Myth

It will be apparent from the previous chapter that the working myth is a powerful factor in the way in which any residential establishment works. This chapter sets out to examine what a working myth is, and how it is arrived at in practice.

MEANING OF THE TERM

The idea of the working myth is itself a myth. That is to say, it does not have any 'real' existence, although for something that does not 'really' exist, it is very powerful! The working myth is the professional counterpart of the 'mental map' people hold in their heads that tells them the way around their building or their neighbourhood; it is a necessary form of shorthand. It is not 'unscientific' or 'unprofessional' to have a working myth. Indeed, being 'scientific' or being 'professional' are in themselves working myths. No criticism is implied of anyone for having or using a working myth, although one may wish to be critical of the *content* of a particular myth.

For present purposes, a working myth is defined as: *The set of assumptions that appear to be held by participants in the work of a residential establishment about what they are doing which influence their day-to-day practice.*

Why Call It a 'Myth'?

It has fallen to anthropologists to try to define the nature of myth, and their definitions fit in some respect with the way in which the term is used here, but not in others. In common parlance a 'myth' is something that is false. That is *not* implied in this discussion, except insofar as any model, however sophisticated, is an inadequate description of the complexity of what it describes. In fact, I could have used the term 'theory' to describe the same phenomenon, but a working myth is a rather special type of theory, and the phrases 'working theory' or 'practice theory', which have been used in other contexts, do not carry the same connotations as I wish to give it. (The closest terminology is Argyris and Schön's 'theory in use' (1974).) 'Model', used by some writers and by myself earlier on in this book for other kinds of description, is not quite appropriate either, because it has connotations of something too formal and thought-out, whereas the working myth is likely to be the indirect product of a conscious model of practice.

Unprovability

First, a myth is *unproven*. It may indeed be *unprovable*. It has this in common with all theories: the philosophy of science is full of debates about the status of theories, and it is held by many workers in the field that although a theory about something can be *dis*proven, it can never by conclusively proven (Popper 1974). It always remains provisional, merely awaiting the experiment that will come along and falsify it. Theoretically if a theory is disproven by experiment, it should be abandoned at once; in practice the theory of science demonstrates that this is far from the case (Kuhn 1970). If the theory is well established, it is more likely that some means will be found to explain away the inconvenient results of the experiment. In this sense theories, even in science, tend to behave like myths, because a myth is something that survives or persists despite evidence against it. If the evidence becomes overwhelming, it might be decided in some sections of the community that 'really' the myth is about something different from what everyone had previously thought it was about, but it persists as a powerful account of whatever it described. Thus, when the combined onslaught of the theory of evolution and the evidence of geology showed that the story of Adam and Eve could not be a scientifically accurate account of the beginnings of humankind, theologians (on the whole) set to and revised their understanding of the first chapters of Genesis. The book now became an account of how humankind reached its present moral, rather than biological, state. The Adam and Eve myth is not necessarily weakened by the discovery that it does not apply 'scientifically'; indeed, the discovery of the proper context in which to understand a myth is necessary to get the most out of it.

So myths tend to persist despite evidence against them.

Usefulness

Second, the most important requirement of a myth is that it should be *useful*. Again, this applies to theories as we use them in everyday life. Even in the scientific community, the way to decide between two competing theories in the absence of experimental validation of one at the expense of another is on the basis of which is the more 'elegant'. Generally speaking this means that one prefers that which accounts for the most experimental data with the smallest amount of theory (using the test of Occam's Razor). It is possible to describe the movement of the planets on the basis of a Ptolemaic (*i.e.* Earth-centred) view of the universe; but it can be done much more simply by a Copernican (sun-centred) model of the solar system. In some cases, where competing theories are equally useful for different purposes, scientists hang on to both of them and accept that there is a paradox in doing so. The most obvious example is in the wave and particle theories of light. Nevertheless, hard-headed people hang on to disproven theories if they remain useful for specific purposes. Surveyors, for example, behave *as if* the Earth were flat; its spherical shape is of no interest at the scale at which they are working, and can be ignored.

One of the problems of theory in social work is that it tends to answer questions that no one is asking, and is therefore seen as useless and may tend to be distrusted. But theory of some kind is absolutely necessary to the process of thinking at all, and so practitioners have a tendency to leave aside the academic theories they have acquired in college or out of books like this one, and to fall back on other 'common-sense' theories that may not be accurate but are at least useful. Such common-sense theories, in which usefulness becomes the major criterion for assessment, are what I am calling 'myths'.

One of the questions worth asking about such myths is, 'Just what are they useful *for*?'

Accuracy

Third, it is desirable for a theory to be *accurate*. As I have shown, even in the scientific community, this does tend to come a poor second to usefulness, but in the case of the myth it comes even further behind that. Whereas a scientific theory may be abandoned if it lacks accuracy despite being attractive and useful, a myth can be woefully inaccurate but in many cases it will only be abandoned when it fails to be useful for anything at all. It is this difference in priority between usefulness and accuracy that distinguishes a myth from a scientific theory. (Just to put another term in context, one might say that an ideology is a myth writ large, see Mannheim 1954.)

Richness

Fourth, a myth is generally a *story*. There is nothing in conceptual, natural, or social science that can ever approach the richness and suggestiveness of a story. After all, a story is an account of something that is alleged to have happened, and thus it is the raw material that theory is brought in to interpret. This can be done in many ways, and none of the interpretations can totally account for or exhaust the material. We can view the Adam and Eve story in terms of palaeontology, morality, theology, psychology, ecology, or even anti-feminism, and probably in many more ways. Moreover, in general conversation, only intellectuals indulge in arguments about what they believe, as theories. Most other people express their beliefs indirectly, through recounting their own or other people's experiences and putting interpretations on them through the way they tell them. The story is a much older form of expression than the abstract theory, appeals to more people, and is frequently more powerful and more persuasive.

The mythic quality comes out in residential practice in the

way in which staff tell each other stories about what happened, or what a particular resident did, which they do much more often than they deliberately spell out the principles on which they work. To a lesser extent the mythic quality also appears when policy decisions are made, as they usually are, by reference to particular instances and problems that have arisen. Rarely are principles laid down in advance and in abstract and then applied directly to situations; generally the reverse is true, in that the principles emerge from numerous examples of practice, and this is how new members of staff and new residents pick up an inarticulate idea of how things are run.

Strictly speaking, this fourth quality of the myth is not fully respected in this discussion, because it is impossible to discuss the underlying principles solely by referring to stories all the time, but it is included here as a reminder that it is the medium by which the working myth is communicated to colleagues and residents.

Inarticulacy

We describe someone as inarticulate when they are unable to express themselves – when they cannot find the words to say what they feel. The term is used in exactly the same sense here. It is not meant as a criticism of the communications skills of either staff or residents, but simply as a description of ideas that people know about at the back of their minds, but which they either find difficult to spell out, or which it never occurs to them to spell out. Such ideas are not unconscious, because they are instantly recognized (although sometimes denied) when they are put to the person who holds them. They may indeed be elicited in conversation if exactly the right questions are asked, but the person who expresses them often seems surprised to find himself saying something that it had never before occurred to him to express in such terms. In a sense, our inarticulate ideas are half-way between conscious and unconscious. There is a term in psychoanalysis to describe this status – 'pre-conscious' – but that is usually applied to memories, and I am concerned with 'ideas at the back of the mind', so 'inarticulate' is preferred. It is in the nature of working myths that they are inarticulate.

THE EXPRESSION OF THE WORKING MYTH

The working myth at its simplest takes the form of: 'We work with people in here *as if* they were . . . and that makes us . . .'. (There is also a common variation of the form: 'We work here as if we were . . . and that makes our clients . . .', in which the definition of the staff role comes first.)

The 'as if' element is important. The reason why a working myth is needed in the first place is the difficulty of making sense of a residential establishment just as it is. It is a peculiar environment, with consequent peculiar roles and relationships, and in broad terms, people are not very good at adapting to completely novel environments. They may without too much difficulty be able to take on board specific novel tasks or perspectives, but a whole living and working environment is difficult to adjust to. It leads to disorientation, and the desire to find familiar landmarks and certainties, even if these are not fully warranted by the situation itself – hence the importance of having a *useful* myth.

Role Paradigms

In many cases what people do under these circumstances is to attempt to 're-make' the confusing environment in the form of something that is familiar or better understood, often a situation where the role relationships are clear-cut and predictable. (These situations can be referred to as 'paradigm' relationships or situations.)

Such an inappropriate paradigm is regularly seen on adult education courses, when the last experience of education many participants have had was at school. Sometimes it takes trivial forms, such as course members putting up their hands when they want to answer a question or make a point – they soon become aware of what they are doing and laugh at themselves.

But sometimes it becomes more serious, when course members cannot grasp that it *is* acceptable to express one's own views in written assignments, and indeed is expected – which contrasts with other schooling experiences in which pupils were expected simply to regurgitate what the teacher said.

One of the problems experienced in some of the more progressive psychiatric hospitals is to do with the expectations which accompany the labels of being 'patient' or 'nurse'. Psychiatric nurses find it an uphill struggle (a Sisyphean task) to get patients to realise that *they* have to work to get better, and that the traditional patient role of lying in bed while medical staff do things to them does not apply. Nurses may well abandon their uniforms and other outward signs of their traditional role in an attempt to convey that this is a new situation with new expectations.

The role of care assistant is difficult for many old people to understand when they come into an elderly person's home. Some of them may slip into the 'patient–nurse' paradigm, to the extent of hailing a care assistant by calling for 'Nurse!'. Others may choose a 'mistress–maid' paradigm, in which they see the care assistants as at their personal beck and call, which understandably irritates many staff. Still others may regard care staff as if they were volunteers, rather like the friendly neighbours who might have looked in on them before they came into residence: in this paradigm they are continually apologising for being such a trouble to the staff, and the reassurance 'But that's what we're here for!' does not seem to get through. The latter residents are of course much more popular.

Some old people are afraid of old people's homes even now because they see them as 'the workhouse'.

A few years ago, when there was a TV series about Colditz prisoner-of-war camp, many young people in care began to refer to their establishment – only half in jest – as 'Colditz'.

In the examples above, the consumers are the ones who generate a myth in the form of a false paradigm about the appropriate relationships. Note that the examples get progressively further removed from actual familiarity. All participants in adult education have at one time been school pupils, and so the regression quoted is not at all surprising. Many psychiatric patients will have some experience of having been general patients, and certainly some experience of participation in the medical system, so their parallels are also understandable, particularly in view of the labels of 'patient' and 'nurse'. The same might go for the elderly resident treating the care assistant as a nurse. But it is less likely that she would ever have had a maid, and to all but the confused it must also be clear that care assistants do quite different things from neighbours. The workhouse disappeared before most residents were even middle-aged, and Colditz was not in the direct experience of any of the young people – it was not even in their lifetime.

The characteristic of all these resident paradigms, however, is that they have clearly defined role expectations. One of the more general problems of social work is that the social worker–client role system is not familiar to the vast majority of people, and they do not know how to take up the role of client (which of course creates uncertainty for the social worker, who may then quite understandably not know how to take up her role). We know what to expect when confronted by a doctor, or a teacher, or a policeman, or a clergyman – but a social worker? Perhaps one of the reasons why social work has such a bad press is because no one (social workers and policy-makers included) is very clear about what social workers distinctively *do*. Perhaps what is needed is a TV series to provide appropriate paradigms.

Staff Paradigms

Staff have less excuse for re-forming perceptions to fit with paradigms, but more reason to do so. They have less excuse in that they are supposed to be 'professional', guided by principles that emphasize the inalienable individuality of each person, and respect for that individuality. But they have more reason in that part of the natural tendency of residential work (the Shell tendency, as we shall later explore it) is to assume responsibility *for* (rather than simply *to*) the residents, and that this imposes an almost intolerable burden. Menzies' classic study (1967) explored the implications of this situation in the nursing context, and then identified the defence mechanisms used both by individual nurses and the system of which they were a part to minimize the emotional impact of such responsibility. To quote T. S. Eliot again, 'Mankind cannot bear very much reality'.

Staff members have specific things to *do* with and for residents, such as bathing, toileting, and lifting, or training, disciplining, and counselling them, but what is difficult if not impossible to specify is:

1. How to respond to this person while one is engaged in this task – does one chat merrily while toileting, or does one do it quietly, impersonally?

2. When to do the various tasks – does this resident need to be controlled at this moment, or can she be left alone? Is this a problem with which he needs help, or can he cope on his own?

One might claim that long-standing acquaintance with a particular resident provides answers to such questions, but in many cases this appears not to be the case. The demands for uniformity of treatment that are enshrined in the procedures of the establishment, and the power of the myths to pre-judge answers to the questions, mean that the frame of reference within which the problems are understood becomes fixed early on both in the career of the staff member and in the relationship with the resident.

What staff members need are guidelines in the back of their minds as they go about their daily tasks, which provide workable answers to the questions, and which therefore preserve them from having to engage too closely with the experience of the residents, because such engagement could paralyse them.

A student on a child care course was placed at a Community Home with Education for her first placement. All her previous experience had been with physically handicapped children (a group with which other students found it traumatic to work). To most observers, the position of the adolescents in the CH(E) would seem infinitely better than that of children with spina bifida or cerebral palsy or brittle bones, but the student was horrified by their plight. She poured out her feelings when the tutor visited: 'What is going to become of them? They've ruined their lives, ending up in here!'. She was in a sense impervious to the tragedies of the lives of her usual clients, but she was vulnerable to the lesser tragedies of the residents of the CH(E). It was not until the placement was almost at an end that she showed any of the considerable talent she had for communicating and working with young people.

In part the student had developed defences to enable her to work with her physically handicapped clients, but in part she could also empathize with them. With the young delinquents in the CH(E) she had neither the defences nor the learned empathy. Some client groups are more difficult to empathize with than others, although they may command a great deal of sympathy. With these groups, too, staff tend to fall back on stereotyped paradigms that make sense to them.

A member of an In-Service course who worked in an Adult Training Centre for people with a mental handicap always referred to his clients as 'kids' – to the extent that other members of the group had come to believe that he worked with children. When confronted with this usage, he said that it was the only way in which he could think about them, because he had no idea what their experience of the world was like, and, 'anyway, they are just like kids, aren't they?'

The answer to his question was clearly 'No!', but having found a paradigm which he could relate to, he held on to it despite pressure to do otherwise. In some limited respects, of course, he was right, but the characteristic of a paradigm is its tendency towards 'nothing but-ism'. Like any stereotype, it tends to ignore evidence that does not confirm it; and where staff are in a position of power, and initiate actions at least as often as they respond to them, there is a tendency to create self-fulfilling labelling patterns.

THE GENESIS OF THE MYTH

We have seen something of the reasons why working myths are powerful and even necessary for many staff, but the important question for the practitioner is how to change them if one does not like them. This is easier said than done, as the previous chapter has suggested, but in order to attempt it at all it is necessary first to have an idea about how they come to take the form they do in one's own particular establishment. Figure 6.1 shows the basic pattern of myth creation.

Figure 6.1 The cycle that creates and maintains the working myth

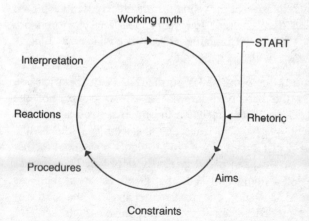

Start

'Start' is not part of the circle because it is not part of the cycle, in the sense that it is not amended or affected by previous stages as the cycle goes round and round as time goes by. The Start refers to the initial conditions within which the residential establishment comes to exist at all. Very occasionally it is the vision of one person or of a small group. Hawkspur Camp was the vision of what was then the Institute for the Scientific Study of Delinquency, Finchden Manor the vision of George Lyward, the Richmond Fellowship that of Elly Jansen, and so on. More often the start is a bureaucratic decision, and it has to be borne in mind that from that initial decision follow a series of lesser decisions that nonetheless set the boundaries within which subsequent developments can take place. Let us take a typical scenario.

Based on research reports into population trends, the Social Services Department of a local authority realizes that there is no way in which its present provision for the elderly will keep pace with demand over the next few years. The Director therefore effectively tells the Committee, 'We need a new Elderly Persons' Home with, say, 36 beds.'

At this stage in the proceedings all that has been specified is a response to the perceived need of a client group. For the moment, because of our focus on the internal processes of the establishment, we have to leave out of account all the factors that led to a decision being made to provide a residential facility rather than, say, expand home care provision. The Director has also suggested a number of beds, partly no doubt on the basis of anticipated demand, and partly perhaps on the basis of government guidelines about the maximum desirable size for such an establishment. The proposal already contains a value judgement that will influence what goes on inside the establishment when it is built.

There is some debate both within the Department and the Committee as to whether this ought to be an establishment for a part of the overall client group (perhaps elderly people with mental infirmities) or a straightforward Part III home. There is also discussion as to whether it ought to include a day centre or an extended kitchen to service the meals-on-wheels service, where it ought to be built within the area, and whether it ought to be group-living based or not. Decisions are finally made, and the framework having been set up, the commission is passed to the Architect's Department and to the Staffing Section to get on with it.

The stage is now set, in rather more detail than one might have thought. The building the architect comes up with will in large measure dictate just what can go on inside it. Converting an establishment for group living if it was never built for it, for example, is very difficult. And it is worth noting that although the architect will consult members of the Social Services Department about requirements, it is usual for the building to be almost finished before the staff are appointed, so the new Officer-in-Charge can have a say only in minor details if at all.

The staffing section will look up the recommended staffing ratios for the proposed establishment (in light of the budget) and will first advertise for an Officer-in-Charge at the standard rate for an establishment of that size.

A further influential decision has now been made: that this establishment will have an 'Officer-in-Charge'. It is by no means necessarily a bad decision, but it does preclude a whole series of other options, such as the establishment being 'satellited' to another one, or having an equally graded team of senior staff, or a team leader of some kind whose job includes some field- or community-based work. I have also deliberately used the term 'Officer-in-Charge', rather than 'Head of Home' or 'Community Leader' or 'Home Manager' – the term used and the job description that goes with it again necessarily limit the options.

The newly appointed Officer-in-Charge is now enlisted in interviewing the rest of her team, including three Deputy Officers-in-Charge, and, close to opening day, Care Assistants, many of whom will work for just 20 hours per week.

Again, there are a host of assumptions built into this structure – about the needs for deputies and the nature of their jobs, about having two kinds of 'professional' staff, one salaried and office based and the others manually graded, part-time and 'floor' based. Such a structure is not quite as immutable as the bricks and mortar of the building, but it will take a lot of time, trying, and trauma to get it changed if it ever needs to be.

Even before any residents have appeared, circumstances and necessary decisions have to a considerable extent shaped what can possibly happen within the new establishment. If the standard scenario is carried through, cooks and domestic staff will be appointed, thereby implying a division of labour within the establishment, which may or may not prove to make sense in the light of subsequent experience.

Rhetoric

Rhetoric is the language of ideals. It is not fair to see it simply as 'empty words', but it does to a large extent affect the terms within which a debate or discussion or decision-making process is conducted. In the case under discussion, the rhetoric is often supplied by outsiders. The opening ceremony of the new establishment is carried out by a visiting dignitary (usually about six months after the place opens in order to fit in with his busy schedule, and in the presence of a group of staff and bemused residents who can't see why anyone should 'open' what is self-evidently already 'open'.) The dignitary utters a few platitudes, and the mayor also has a word, saying: 'We should all like to thank the Officer-in-Charge and her team for having done so much in such a short time to create such a homely atmosphere, as we have seen today.'

'We hope that this Home will not only be a comfortable and friendly place for old people to spend their final years, but also a symbol to everyone else of a caring community.'

Such sentiments may be naïve, and the reference to 'final years' may not go down too well with some of the residents, but the terminology of 'homeliness', 'comfort', and 'friendship' sets the tone of the ideal expectations on the part of the outside world, which may well resist any attempt to re-define the culture in terms of, for example, stimulation, external involvement, or even rehabilitation. What the establishment symbolizes to outsiders is also important, because it means that any publicized attempt to do things differently may call forth considerable resistance.

Aims

If the rhetoric embodies external expectations, the aims of the establishment embody the internal intentions – the original values of the staff (at this stage). They are often expressed in the literature sent to prospective job applicants and perhaps to prospective residents, or in the kind of thing the Officer-in-Charge says when introducing the Home: 'What we are trying to do here is to create a homely atmosphere – we like to think that residents will feel that it is indeed their *home.*'

With a little reflection, practically anyone can point out that this aim is not realizable in practice. By comparison with living in one's own house, with all the freedom of choice (and indeed the responsibility) that implies, life in a 'home' for elderly people comes off a very poor second. That, however, does not invalidate the aim. The aim is a statement of *direction*, rather than a statement about a point that may realistically be reached. The values behind the establishment are very close to the surface in statements of aim.

Constraints

So far, the rhetoric and the aims have been speaking about an ideal world. But very soon the limitations of practicality are reached.

> We should like residents to bring as much of their furniture as possible with them, but unfortunately the rooms are very small.

> I don't think it's really practical to allow residents to cook for themselves – for one thing there's nowhere except the

main kitchens, and for another some of them are not safe with pans full of hot food – and if we allow one to do it we'd have to allow all of them to.

I agree that residents should be encouraged to do their own shopping at the local shops – but they are about half a mile away and we haven't got the staffing to accompany them whenever they want to go, so I think we'll just have to settle for care staff or volunteers running errands, and a trolley.

If politics is the art of the possible, so is residential work. Compromise is unavoidable, even when there is the kind of commitment to the embodiment of values in practice that was discussed in the previous chapter. Values, however, are continually present in the way in which the constraints are perceived. Implicit in the second example quoted, for example, is the assumption that what goes for one resident must go for them all, which is one understanding of 'fairness'. Weighing the interests of the individual against those of the group is another perpetual dilemma of residential practice.

Procedures

What happens in practice is the product of compromise between the aims and the constraints, and every practitioner, particularly those in management positions, is familiar with the process of working out such a compromise. As discussed in the previous chapter, sometimes the answer comes out at the level of administrative convenience, and sometimes extra effort, either on the part of the staff at large or on the part of the Head of Home fighting for increased resources, results in a compromise that is closer to the aims than that.

We should like the residents to have free use of their rooms all day, but the domestic staff need to get in at some time to clean, and their hours are strictly scheduled – so we have to tell people they have to be out of their rooms between 10 o'clock and lunch-time, but they can go in at any other time.

Clearly residents ought to be able to choose which clothes

they want to wear, but some of them would put on the same soiled dress every day – so care assistants have to remove that day's clothes to the laundry every night.

I suppose residents do have a right to have alcoholic drink whenever they like if they can afford it – but with some of them it clashes with medication, and the doctor and the Department would be down on us if we allowed anyone to get ill like that. So if they are on any medication like that, we have to insist that we look after any alcohol they may have until they have finished the course of treatment,

It is interesting to note that frequently such 'rules' are interpreted by residents, and by staff who have not been properly inducted, as being much stricter than they really are: 'We're not supposed to go into our rooms during the day'; 'We have to wear the clothes the care staff put out for us'; 'Alcohol is not allowed in here.' And there is often little overt complaint about them (Clough 1981).

Reactions

That brings us to the next stage in the cycle, the reactions that follow from the procedures. Sometimes procedures just do not work.

We did try a choice of menu at one time. But because we can't afford to waste food, we had to use one of those systems where you choose what you want for the next day's meals in advance. Some of the residents forgot what they had ordered, and some of them expected it for the next meal instead of the next day's meal, and some of them kept deciding what their neighbour had was nicer than theirs and said they were being unfairly treated – so we gave up.

That possibility shades into the next one, that staff (or residents) are not willing to put in the effort to make them work:

We tried having a residents' committee, but it was difficult getting the residents to take enough interest to take up their places on it, and the ones who did were really self-appointed rather than elected. The only thing which seemed to interest *them* was having a bar, and really that would have involved too much hassle with the Department and it only interested a minority anyway. So when I finally said it could not be done they seemed to lose interest and the committee just sort of faded away.

Sometimes procedures are actively resisted:

When we first opened, I was determined to get away from that line of chairs around the walls, and so we put them in small circles to encourage residents to talk to each other. Do you know, they actually pushed them back to the walls? Some of them fell over trying to push them.

When such things happen, and there is no consultative machinery within the establishment, it is very difficult to know whether one ought to persist because ultimately more intimate groupings will be 'better for' the residents, or whether to respect their apparent wishes. In the event, it appears that such questions are often decided by what is more administratively convenient for the staff.

Interpretations

Growing experience with procedures and reactions leads to anticipation of how any new ideas will be reacted to: 'They don't want to be bothered with other residents'; 'It's pathetic, really – I don't think they'd notice or complain if you gave them dry bread and water for their tea.' By this stage in the cycle there is a growing body of common-sense interpretation of the routine events and behaviour in the establishment, and such understandings are shared informally among members of the staff in such a way that they command general assent. Expressing such views or values becomes a sort of password for admission to the social world of the staff group.

These interpretations in the light of previous experience then come to be applied to new events, whether they are appropriate or not.

> Well, this new care assistant came along to me and asked where she could get a wheelchair from. I asked who it was for and she said Mr D. So I told here not to pay any attention to him; he's always trying to con staff into pushing him about. He can walk all right if he has to.

Arthritis can vary in painfulness from day to day, but it is difficult for staff to assess every situation on its merits, and so standing 'recipes' evolve that are applied to all superficially similar situations – either Mr D. can always walk or he can never walk. If Mrs E can hear you talking across the room, she can hear you when you stand in front of her and speak more quietly. But being hard of hearing plays funny tricks. Disability may be interpreted as wilful non-cooperation or manipulation; feeble attempts to assert individuality as deliberate attempts to annoy; polite smiles as real expressions of contentment, and so on.

The Working Myth itself

And so the working myth is developed. The specific interpretations of the meanings of behaviour and the characteristics of individual residents become generalized into a set of considerations that can be held in the mind of the staff member about 'what people in here are like'. From 'what people in here are like' it is a short step to 'what people in here need is . . .' and hence to 'my job is . . .''.

What has actually happened is that a set of *technical* considerations about the needs of the residents and the capacity of the establishment to respond to them has been developed into a *moral* categorization - from observations about what *is* the case, we have moved to ideas about what *ought* to be the case in practice.

Round and Round

The first trip around the cycle is a stumbling process, and the myth that emerges is fragile and provisional – it just takes one or two bits of contrary evidence to destroy it. From the original rhetoric and formulation of aims, realization of constraints, and development of procedures to getting reactions to those procedures may be a matter of weeks, and if interpretations and myths have not been imported into the system of the new residential establishment from outside (possibly by staff with experience elsewhere coming to work there) they are slow to develop. Once they do develop, they in turn affect the rhetoric and the aims. Old constraints are confirmed and new ones discovered. Procedures are revised, both at the policy level and in routine practice, possibly accommodating crises and unusual events. These are reacted to in turn, and everyone arrives at their interpretations and the myth is modified. The cycle repeats itself in a matter of days, and then in hours. Rather like a roundabout gathering speed, in which distinct features in slow motion begin to blur into each other as it goes faster and faster, the cycle becomes subject to less and less variation, and the working myth is confirmed by more and more apparent evidence with every cycle. In a few weeks or months it is so established that it seems impossible to change it. This is first-order change working at a high order of efficiency.

The Effects of Crises

Crises have been mentioned above, and they deserve a little elaboration. The southern region of British Rail (now known as 'Network South-East') is one of the most intensively used rail systems in the world, and so commuters are given to asking why fares are so high. The answer lies in the patterns of usage of the trains. Practically all the passengers are carried during the peak rush hours of the morning and late afternoon, and therefore the system has to have enough trains, track, and other resources including staff to cope with the peaks, although most of it is idle for most of the day and night. In a different area, large civil engineering structures such as bridges have to be designed to cope with abnormally high loads and abnormal weather conditions such as 70 to 100 m.p.h. gales, which they may only encounter in practice every three years or so. This makes them very expensive. In social systems it is a moot point to what extent they ought to be designed to cope with such peaks of abnormal pressure, and that depends to a certain extent on the assessment of the risks. Fire precautions provide a good example. Should people in residential establishments be subject to routine inconvenience by sets of fire doors and the distinctly 'unhomely' presence of fire extinguishers on the walls and detectors on the ceilings simply to cope with the relatively unlikely occurrence of fire? Most managers, mindful of their accountability for the physical well-being and safety of the residents, would have to say yes.

Procedures are often formulated in residential establishments in response to problems that have occurred in that, or a similar, establishment in the past, despite the fact that they are not very likely to occur again.

In an old people's home, the doors to individual rooms were locked all day until residents went to bed. Only the senior officer on duty had the keys and had to be called if a resident ever wanted to go into their room. The locking had initially been instituted when there were several residents given to wandering into other people's rooms and taking things. At that time all care assistants had keys, but then there had been some evidence of pilfering. The wandering residents and the pilfering staff member had long since gone, but the locking continued.

Theoretically the justification for this was that it could happen again, but it could have been abandoned and rapidly brought back into operation if it ever proved necessary. A more persuasive explanation was that of sheer inertia, backed by the fit with the working myth, which had been unduly influenced by the crisis.

The relevance of the crisis issue to the working myth at the general level is that planning for crises is based on a 'worst possible case' scenario, which represents the most pessimistic view of human nature, thereby indicating a working myth that stresses the needs, weaknesses, and disabilities of the residents at the expense of their strengths and capabilities (see also the section on redundancy in Chapter 2).

MULTIPLE MYTHS

We have examined a simple case of the creation of a working myth, although its exact formulation has not been spelt out. We have seen that such a myth is a set of assumptions, and that it is rarely explored explicitly. It follows from this that it is something that new staff and residents 'pick up' rather than learn as a result of a formal induction period, and it is not therefore surprising if occasionally they pick it up differently. In many cases staff seem to pick up variations on a fairly common theme, and the variations are not significant except perhaps in fairly specialized circumstances.

There are, however, occasions on which different subgroups within the staff acquire quite different working myths, and this causes perpetual problems, which are rarely dealt with at source precisely because the myth itself is inarticulate. Instead, attention is directed at specific incidents handled in ways at variance with the myth espoused by the senior staff of the establishment, and those staff wonder why when one incident is cleared up other similar ones arise and there is little evidence of any transfer of learning on the part of other staff from one situation to another. Supervision programmes and staff meetings can go on for years dealing with such issues. In its most serious form, the end result is a fragmented staff group at odds with itself and a total loss of any consistency of care.

The roots of the multiple myth problem are basically five, and most occurrences will be found to be variations on one or more of these themes.

1. Staff come from different disciplines and the assumptions behind their training have never been fully confronted and the issues resolved. Perhaps the commonest case relates to nurses coming into social services settings. The essence of

hospital practice is the emphasis on physical care and provision for potential crises; this leads to assumptions about the avoidance of risk that may well be quite at variance with a social work approach, which accepts that risk is an essential element in trying to preserve 'ordinary life'. (This is basically an aspect of the Shell versus Skeleton debate; see Chapter 8.) In many cases it is possible to clarify the situation as long as it is done while the former nurse is somewhat unsure of herself shortly after she joins the team. If, however, the issue is not picked up and she gets used to using her nursing perspective as well as her skills, the problem can become entrenched. Less frequently similar problems may be encountered with former teachers or policemen, or anyone whose previous discipline involved a clear paradigm of role relationships.

One student on a qualifying course had come into social work from a lengthy period as a life insurance salesman. He had considerable problems on placement, and when pushed about his values in a follow-up tutorial he presented his view of child care as, 'I'm in the job of selling the lads a better way of life'. This fitted closely with his working pattern, which involved rapid establishment of seemingly close relationships with boys in a CH(E) – in a way which was the envy of some of his colleagues – followed by equally rapid rejection of them if they did not respond whole-heartedly to all his advice and 'selling technique'. To all intents and purposes he treated them as potential customers, and like any good salesman he did not waste time with people who were not good prospects. He found the culture of the training programme so alien that he became convinced the tutors were trying to 'brainwash' him and left the course.

2. Where there are different disciplines represented within the establishment as a whole, and especially where they have their own hierarchies, multiple myths are very common, and indeed are recognized as such. The clearest case used to be in Community Homes with Education, where there may well have been social work staff, academic teachers, and

instructors in three almost separate but parallel working systems. Tensions became particularly evident with teaching staff doing their 'extraneous duties' – assisting in the house units in the evenings or weekends. They had often established quite different relationships with their pupils in the classroom from those which house staff had made in the living quarters, and both teachers and pupils found it difficult to adjust to the changes of role. The problem might be further compounded by the overall authority of the usually unqualified house staff on their own territory being resented by the more highly trained and highly paid teachers – which militated against any open exploration of the differences of approach.

3. Where cohesive shift teams develop strong team identities over and against the establishment as a whole, and because they consistently work together, they have very little contact with their counterparts on other shifts. This can lead to destructive oscillations between, say, authoritarian and permissive regimes, depending on which team is on duty. The psychological features of this system are such that polarization and splitting tend to develop between the subgroupings, and they can only be reorganized at the cost of an extended period of confusion, disaffection, low morale, and resentment of management for breaking up their cosy cliques. A similar pattern can be detected in relations between night and day staff in some homes for elderly people.

4. Where a new member of staff has been inducted by the usually admirable process of pairing her with an established member, but in this case one who is not quite 'sound' as far as the working myth goes. Modelling is a powerful process, and if the new member is also continually exposed to the anecdotes and grumbles of the older staff, each of which carries its own mythic message, she is likely to internalize or pick up these values rather than those of the rest of the establishment. For this reason it appears that trying to get a member of staff to integrate by giving her the responsibility for the induction of an impressionable new member is a dangerous strategy.

5. Where the motivation of some staff is primarily instrumental, that is they are working for the money, and perhaps because it is a part time occupation that fits in with their family commitments. In such cases the life of the residential community may not be important enough to them for them to be influenced by the more professional values of senior staff and more committed colleagues. They will seek and create a myth that facilitates their survival without any necessary engagement with the residents. It may be indulgent, it may be oppressive or even abusive, and it may well be unfair in the sense of having favourites among the residents. It may draw naïvely on their own experience of having brought up a family, and sometimes it is 'better' than the 'official' myth. Whatever its nature, it is likely to be primarily concerned with short-term solutions to inconvenient situations and not to go beyond the 'order' step on the staircase (Chapter 4).

INTERACTION OF MULTIPLE MYTHS

It is not surprising if the existence of multiple myths leads to recurring disagreements within the establishment, and limits the possibility of developing a cohesive team, but the interactions can be more complex than that.

Lack of Communication

One relatively mild possibility is that there is a total lack of communication between the holders of the different myths. There may be a great deal of talking, but because the disagreements are so profound there is no understanding. Walter (1978) discovered such a situation in his investigation of a List D school in Scotland (corresponding roughly to a Community Home with Education). There was much talk between the staff and the boys about their 'problems', but the same word was defined quite differently by the two groups. The staff believed that the boys were at the school because of their problems; and that when their problems were resolved, they would go home. The boys, on the other hand, saw the fact that they were at the school as their problem, and that once they went home, their problem would be resolved. Walter notes, however, that the boys were aware of the staff myth about them, and believed that by conforming to it, they could achieve their objective of going home – but without having any belief in what the staff thought they were doing with or for them.

In this case a sort of phoney accommodation was reached between the two groups, fundamentally because of the boys' recognition of the staff power to grant or withhold their objective. Where there is a pronounced power differential, such strategies of 'going through the motions' or 'keeping your nose clean' are not uncommon. There is a benign variation in more overtly 'caring' establishments. As one resident put it in a unit for people with physical disabilities:

> The staff like to think that they are providing a 'home' for us. They don't live here, so they don't really know what it's like. But we know that they have a difficult job, and if it helps them to believe that that is what they are doing, that's all right by us.

In other words, the residents indulge the staff fantasies, as they see them.

Polarization

A more destructive pattern, found more commonly in more equally matched groups, is the progressive polarization of positions. The areas of disagreement between policies or beliefs frequently stand out more clearly than areas of agreement, regardless of the setting or context. Working myths are never perfect, and cannot provide totally adequate accounts of what goes on in any establishment, simply because they are generalized. The temptation is to blame believers in a different myth for the failure of one's own, setting up the 'If it weren't for you . . .' game. The fundamental dynamic of this process is *projection*, in which aspects of oneself that one is not prepared to own are externalized and found in other people, so that they can be rejected, criticized, and complained about (see Chapter 2). It is rare for differences to be valued and celebrated, and particularly so when the issue over which people differ is important for their psychological survival. Moreover, the less secure one's own belief, the more it can be bolstered by projection of its failings onto others.

In one child care establishment, the two opposing myths could roughly be summarised as the view that the children were 'deprived' (held by the Officer-in-Charge), and that they were 'depraved' (held by his Deputy). Some staff were clearly in one camp or the other, and some were simply confused and sought various ways out. It proved impossible to contain the conflicting views, and over a period of about eighteen months the two senior staff saw less and less of each other and resorted to communication by memo. At length the Officer-in-Charge delivered an ultimatum to the management of the Department – if the Deputy was not transferred, he would resign. His bluff was called, and it was he who went.

The Officer-in-Charge was sustained in his view of the children as victims by the way in which he saw his Deputy dealing with them, while the Deputy was confirmed in his view of them as junior criminals by the way in which they seemed to exploit the 'soft' regime. The third element in this destructive system, of course, was provided by the staff and the children, who had an unacknowledged but powerful interest in splitting the two senior staff because of the opportunities such a split created for them to do as they liked.

CONCLUSION

In this chapter I have set out the nature of the working myth, without going into great detail about its content – that is the province of the next chapter. However, a working myth of some kind or another, naïve or sophisticated, helpful or hindering, close to the surface or deeply unconscious, is characteristic of *all* residential establishments (and many other social systems as well). The issue for the practitioner therefore is not whether the myth exists or not, but what form it takes, and whether it is appropriate to the overall task of the establishment. Even administrative convenience is a myth in the sense that it provides an orientation to the work and to the residents, of the order of, 'We work with people in here as if they were not really worth putting ourselves out for', or more kindly, 'as if the establishment as a whole were more important than any of its members'.

7 More about Myths

So far we have looked at the nature of working myths and how they come into being, but we have steered clear of their actual content. In this chapter we shall be concerned with content, but it should be emphasized that these are *examples only*. It would be impossible to give an exhaustive account of the potential varieties of working myths. And since the intention of this book is to help the practitioner in residential work to reflect on some generally neglected aspects of that work, it is better to offer a guide to discovering one's own working myth, rather than a spurious list of categories into which one might try to fit one's own establishment, only succeeding at the cost of violating its unique features. There is one form of myth that seems to be a component in one form or another in practically all others, however: this is the Skeleton and Shell factor, which is explored (expressed in a slightly different form) in the next chapter.

MYTHS ELSEWHERE IN THE LITERATURE

Although the terminology of the working myth applied to this context is mine, the underlying ideas are not particularly original. They appear in slightly different forms by other writers on residential work, notably Miller and Gwynne (1972), Wolfensberger (1982), Clough (1981), and Willcocks, Peace, and Kellaher (1987).

The Horticultural and Warehousing Myths

Miller and Gwynne's study was based on a commission to explore the social system of an establishment for people with physical handicaps (one of the Cheshire Foundation homes), which they compare with other approaches to residential care for such people, including local authority establishments and long-stay hospital wards. The discussion is wide-ranging and too important to attempt to summarize here, but one central element is the distinction between horticultural and warehousing models of provision.

The warehousing approach emphasizes the dependence of the residents to the exclusion of their other attributes, and – when it takes a benevolent form – leads to them being looked after with great care and concern at a physical level. Everything is done for them at that level, but little attention is paid to their social and emotional needs because the concern for their physical dependence obscures such minor features. There is consequently a denial of their status as people, and they are seen rather as precious objects that require constant maintenance and care to ensure that they remain in optimum condition. All risks have to be avoided, and all choice is denied. In the terminology of the next chapter, they are kept in a complete Shell.

The horticultural approach on the other hand (which could perhaps more memorably be called the 'greenhousing' approach), emphasizes the residents' potential rather than their needs, and encourages them to do more and more for themselves each day, to exercise choice and to be independent. Superficially this seems to be the more attractive option, and more in keeping with the rhetoric of many social work, rather than health care, establishments. To a certain extent, although not completely, it fits with the notion of the Skeleton.

Miller and Gwynne point out, however, that the horticultural model can be as destructive as the warehousing one, in that for residents with degenerative disorders, for example, it is a cruel delusion. They are not going to get better and more capable as time goes by; rather, they are likely to become more and more dependent. If the warehousing model rests on a denial of independence, the horticultural one rests on a denial of the reality of dependence.

As an alternative they propose what we may call a *negotiated* model, in which a realistic assessment is made of the balance of dependence and independence appropriate to each resident at a given stage in his life and the progress or remission of his disorder, through sensitive consultation with the person himself, and a living environment is designed accordingly.

The warehousing and horticultural models are working myths, but the negotiated order is not. (It is worth noting that Miller and Gwynne also refer explicitly to myths in residential settings, but that they are referring to much more specific, powerful, but mistaken beliefs about aspects of the social system than the present usage of the term.) The two rejected forms are reflections of actual practices, whereas the recommended alternative is an active philosophy of practice that is to be imposed on what already happens. It is possible that it could attain the status of a working myth in an establishment in which it had operated for some considerable period, but it would have to be introduced and developed at length. The actual myth form it would take would be something like, 'We work with people in here as if they were experts on their own needs, and that makes us . . .'. The latter part is left uncertain; there is no paradigmatic role relationship that is familiar enough to most practitioners to help them understand just *how* they ought to respond to their expert clients. Technician, perhaps, or simple servant?

This is not to suggest that the negotiated model is not a very worthwhile one, but simply that it is not a working myth, and it remains uncertain as to whether it ever will be. It is a *vision*, at the rhetoric/aims stage of the cycle discussed in the last chapter. The working myth is a way of accounting for what happens (based on assumptions about what ought to happen), whereas the vision is essentially a prescriptive one of what *ought* to happen.

Models of Handicap

Wolfensberger is the apostle of 'normalization' as a philosophy of residential provision, particularly for people with a mental handicap. He also draws attention to models of the client that we would identify as working myths, and points out how these are enshrined not merely in the practices of institutions, but also in their physical fabric. (See the early stages in the development of the working myth, p. 113.) He identifies the following models or myths (1982): the retarded person as sick; the retarded person as a subhuman organism; the retarded person as a menace; the retarded person as an object of pity; the retarded person as a burden of charity; the retarded person as a holy innocent; the retarded person as a developing individual. In each case Wolfensberger shows how the assumptions underlying the working myths provide a general orientation towards their task for those working with the clients, and bolster their own identity. As in this study, he suggests that some ideology is inevitable in designing and carrying out programmes of care or provision for disadvantaged groups, making the point that it is not a matter of choosing ideology versus no ideology, but good ideologies versus bad ones, and consciousness of them versus unconsciousness of them. He also follows the sociologists of deviance in exploring how the labelling process affects the clients' own perception of themselves, all of which leads him to the now famous articulation of the principle of normalization. However, like Miller and Gwynne's negotiated model, the normalization principle and its associated myth of the person with a handicap as a developing individual suffers from the lack of a paradigm for the relationship of worker to client. The principle itself declares that *as far as possible* the standards of ordinary society should be normative in the treatment of clients. It thereby provides a reference point against which responses to informed assessments of the capabilities of clients may be judged. It does not declare dogmatically that, for example, 'All people with a mental handicap should live in ordinary housing'. One might say that it does put the onus on those who believe that clients should be treated differently from the norm to prove their point. In many cases, one has to admit, that point is not too difficult to prove – but by making the starting point not a medical, or a custodial, or even a charitable frame of reference, normalization undermines the paradigm relationships of such professional groups and leaves them floundering. It is not surprising, therefore, that normalization tends to surface in a distorted form in some projects (although by no means all), where it finds expression for example in an ill-thought-out obsession with the externals (such as ordinary housing) and an uncertainty about role in those who work with the users.

Activity and Disengagement

If the warehousing and horticultural models are accounts of the relationship between the staff and the residents, and Wolfensberger's models are accounts of the ways in which society has seen its handicapped deviants, the activity and disengagement myths are accounts of differing views of appropriate approaches to old age that may be shared by both residents and staff. Briefly, the activity view holds that a good old age is one in which the person keeps as active as possible and as involved with the world as possible until he or she drops. The disengagement view holds that old age is the time gradually to remove oneself from the hurly-burly of life, to take a well-deserved rest, and to be free from the cares that beset the rest of us; and that this process is one in which both the old person herself and the wider community have a part to play. It can be seen at once that whichever view one takes will profoundly influence the kind of residential provision that is seen as appropriate for elderly people. (Clough (1981) merely provides an accessible summary of the ideas; the models themselves originate from Havighurst and Albrecht (1953) on the activity side, and Cumming and Henry (1961) on the disengagement side. Note that both models are rarely found in a pure form.)

It frequently appears that these myths, which of course have their origin in attitudes to old age at large rather than simply within the residential establishment, command allegiance from different groups within old people's homes. The activity view is more popular among the more 'professional' senior staff, and indeed perhaps the management. They emphasize self-help, choice, independence, and stimulation to keep the residents functioning at as 'high' a level as possible for as long as possible. In many cases, however, maintaining this model as the basis for a working myth seems to be a Sisyphean task – in other words, it is not the *de facto* myth of the establishment at all. Instead, the care assistants and the residents often cling to the disengagement model and effectively resist all attempts to get them to see the situation otherwise. There is a problem here that has both technical and ethical aspects. To what extent is the apparent disengagement view of the residents a product of the fact that they are in the Home, or is it a view that they would be inclined to adopt outside? Twenty years ago, when residents in old people's homes were on the whole less dependent and the decision to enter one appeared to be more of a free choice, this would have been an easier question to answer. People who entered residential establishments did so at least in part because they wised to be freed from the burden of caring for themselves, and thus there was a suggestion that they selected themselves from among those who held the disengagement view – other old people who held the activity view sought to maintain their 'independence' as long as possible. Today, one cannot draw the same conclusions because the growth in domiciliary services on the one hand and the competition for scarce places on the other have meant that as far as the statutory sector is concerned the decision to enter is made on quite different grounds of apparent need. The position today in private establishments on the other hand may be similar to that of twenty years ago in the statutory sector.

It is possible to conceive of ways of gathering evidence to test the above hypothesis, but the ethical question would still remain – by what right do professionals seek to impose an activity model on those who wish for a disengaged old age? It is a paradoxical situation, in which the only choice that the professionals seek to deny to their residents is that of not having to choose!

As the Skeleton and Shell argument will suggest, it is easier to run an establishment for basically passive consumers than for active ones, and therefore there is a further question about whether the seeming adoption of a disengagement model by those working 'on the floor' is in fact motivated as much by considerations of administrative convenience as of conviction as to the desires of the residents themselves. Certainly Miller and Gwynne pay explicit attention to the associated issue of the way in which what we are here calling working myths function as defence mechanisms (drawing on Menzies 1967), and Wolfensberger makes a similar point from a more sociological angle.

Myths in Teaching

It is not only in relation to residential work that ideas corresponding to working myths are found. Hargreaves (1972) identifies three different ones among teachers, whom he represents as *lion tamers*, *entertainers*, or *new romantics*. The lion-tamer is the kind of teacher who believes that the task of teaching is similar to that of getting animals to jump through hoops, because no one wants to learn anything unless they are pushed to do so; he therefore relies strongly on punishment and control to achieve his ends. The entertainer shares his general belief in the unwillingness of pupils to learn, but believes that they will respond as long as learning can be disguised as something else, especially as 'fun'; he therefore goes to great lengths to create interesting exercises and games to keep pupils happy in the hope that some of the learning will rub off on them. The new romantic differs from his colleagues in the belief that there is a natural motivation to learn on the part of the pupils and that all that needs to happen is that this inclination should be given free rein and not be fettered by anything getting in the way.

The reason for bringing in the reference to teachers is that while the entertainer is fairly rare in social work circles (with the possible exception of some workers in intermediate treatment), the lion-tamer and the new romantic have their direct counterparts among policy-makers and practitioners. This is really not surprising, because like many myths, these views have respectable philosophical antecedents that go back almost as far as recorded thought.

MYTHS AND HUMAN NATURE

Reducing the lion-tamer and the new romantic views to their basic elements, we find in one a fundamental conviction that left to themselves people are basically *bad*, and in the other the alternative view that left to themselves people are basically *good*. The question as to which is true is of course unanswerable in any scientific sense, which accounts for the extent to which refuge has often been found in systems of religious or political thought – although it is worthy of note that Christianity, for example, has been believed at different times to be capable of justifying either position. Despite the rhetoric of religious sanction, therefore, it may be more appropriate to see the religious component as a *post hoc* justification for more culturally, politically, and even materially motivated factors.

In the first chapters of Genesis we find that Adam is made 'in the image of God', and that later he and Eve are cursed by sin and cast out from the Garden. The problem of the co-existence of the two strands is to be found even there. Among the relatively early Christian writers (about the fifth century) there is the great dispute between Augustine, propounding the utter depravity of human beings, and Pelagius, suggesting their perfectibility (Bettenson 1943).

But come closer to home and to secular philosophy, and the two strands are represented by Hobbes (1588–1679), who proclaimed in his *Leviathan* that 'the life of man [is] solitary, poor, nasty, brutish and short', and by Rousseau (1712–78), who wrote of the 'noble savage' as the original state of humanity. (It is salutary to note that Hobbes seems to have been a much nicer man than Rousseau, but that the political blueprints following their arguments are not all that different (Russell 1984).) The 'bad' strain seems to have rather died out in respectable philosophy since then, although it remains a social-psychological reality (being a central element in the 'authoritarian personality' (Adorno *et al.* 1983)) and an influential political voice. The 'good', or romantic view, on the other hand finds expression in humanistic psychology, particularly in that which builds on the ideas of Carl Rogers, and in liberal political thought (Rogers 1951).

Little Villains

Any establishment based on the assumption that the people in it are fundamentally 'bad' will always cater for the 'worst possible case' scenario, and put the least charitable interpretation on the conduct of any resident (or member of staff, in many cases).

One working myth that seemed to embody this principle was found in a Community Home with Education, and its more general applicability was confirmed by a number of instances:

The entire day-to-day working of the establishment was based on the belief that left to themselves the 'lads' would be 'up to no good'. This gave the staff a fairly clear and simple role to occupy. It was essential that lads should be supervised at all times; when in doubt, any door should be locked; if an inmate had been home for the weekend or off the site for any reason, he had to be searched for 'contraband' immediately on return.

The regime might be felt to be more suited to a prison that to a supposedly rehabilitative establishment, and indeed the prison probably provided the paradigm for it. The working myth could be summarised as: 'We work with the boys in here as if they were little villains, and that makes us prison officers.' The 'little villains' working myth is a component in other more sophisticated regimes, too – particularly those in which it appears to be believed that when the residents get together, their groupings can only be inimical to the overall values of the establishment (*cf.* Bramham 1980). In that case the variation becomes something like: 'We work with the residents as if they were likely to be dragged down or contaminated by each other, and that makes us 'anti-group' workers.'

Readers familiar with the history of residential establishments will be aware that both of these myths have precedents: the Poor Law of 1834, which established the Oliver Twist kind of workhouse, enshrined similar principles in its attitude to the poor, and the 'silent system' of the Victorian prison was based on a conviction that solitary meditation was the way to assist in the regeneration of the moral sense of the criminal, who could only be further corrupted by his involvement with other prisoners. (As a matter of interest, the same argument was used in the eighteenth century against the very idea of educating young people together in schools (see Musgrove 1964:47).)

In modern terms this set of myths is more likely to be found in child-care establishments than anywhere else, but it has variations in work with other client groups. Its counterpart in work with people with a mental handicap or mental illness, for example, is based on a basic fear of their alleged unpredictability, lack of reason, and potential for violence. It comes down to: 'We work with the residents as if they were dangerous, and that makes us alternately controllers and humourers.' It can be seen that in this view, wariness is all, and the basic 'trick' is to assess whether a resident's conduct is likely to cause further problems for the establishment or not, or whether thwarting him is likely to result in an outburst or not. If no problems are foreseen and especially if an outburst is likely, he will be humoured; if the contrary is true, he will be controlled. In either case there is no consideration of the possibility of reasonableness in the behaviour, or any significance attached to the frustration or other feelings that may well underlie it. To take such considerations on board, of course, is part of the principle of normalization.

Victims

The alternative 'good' construction on human nature can equally be expressed in a variety of working myths, ranging from the naïve to the sophisticated.

The great danger of this group of myths (corresponding to the danger of outright cruelty in the 'bad' group) is idealization of the client, and difficulty in reconciling such an idealized view with the reality of their situation, leading to a splitting process on the part of the staff that comes down to *inside here good*, *outside bad*. The limitations of such a split are clear when it comes to issues of rehabilitation or the mitigation step on the staircase (Chapter 4). Similarly, just as the 'bad' myths find it difficult to get beyond order issues on the staircase, 'good' myths are likely to fall down in not being able to find a rationale for establishing order in the first place.

The myth of goodness is difficult to sustain in its naïve form. Perhaps it is best illustrated in the rhetoric of the old orphanage or the former name of the Church of England Children's Society: Waifs and Strays. It must account for the plight of consumers in terms of their being victims, which casts the staff as rescuers, and crucially creates the expectation of *gratitude* on the part of the users. As many social workers have discovered to their personal disillusionment, users do not tend to be grateful for the services they are offered. Some are, but there is in modern thought no reason for them to be so. Currently, the wisdom is that in receiving residential or other social or health provision, they are getting no more than their rights, and indeed many voices are raised to claim that the rights they get are less than they deserve.

Paradoxically, the victim–rescuer relationship has also historically been used to justify some fairly awful practice, and indeed it can also be adapted so that it accounts not so much for the potential goodness of consumers as for the actual 'goodness' of service providers, in which case it can coexist with a polarized view of the consumer as 'bad'. This of course was the further dynamic of the workhouse and many 'charitable' efforts, and provided a standing excuse for poor provision on the grounds that what the consumers were getting was better than they would have received outside the institution, as in the case of Wolfensberger's 'retarded person as a burden of charity' model.

Even when the belief in the potential goodness of consumers is accepted, they tend to be seen as having been tainted by the outside world, since innocence is a fragile thing, and this too could be used as an argument for beatings and oppression within the institution, since evil has to be driven out by whatever means are to hand.

Therapeutic Communities

Nonetheless, if naïve belief in the inherent goodness of people is prone to distortion, there have been and continue to be other examples based on more sophisticated understandings of the myth. Tuke's 'Retreat' at York at the end of the eighteenth century still stands as a model of care for mentally ill people, believing in a regime of 'moral management', which, although it sounds daunting and oppressive to modern ears, consisted largely in a belief in the curative properties of fresh air, healthy outdoor labour, good wholesome food, and kindness. Kennard's brief sketch of what happened to Tuke's vision (1983) suggests that the moral management regime was to a large extent a victim of its own success. Others took up the idea in a half-baked form and tried to reproduce ever larger institutions of the same kind, ignoring the fact that in Tuke's understanding the maximum size of such an establishment was a total group (including staff) of one hundred; and incidentally trying to apply it to generally poorer and less well educated clients to whom the 'care staff' were less prepared to respond as servants. The servant–master/mistress relationship was the paradigmatic relationship of the Retreat.

More recently the tradition of goodness has become refined into a belief in the potential for growth in each individual, which includes the capacity not only to overcome one's own problems or handicaps, but also the capacity to help others to do so – hence the therapeutic community movements, in which far from seeing other residents as obstacles to development, there is positive encouragement of self-help among the resident community.

Such therapeutic communities, as is implied by their name, have an overall working myth of the order of: 'We work with people in here as if they will grow given the right conditions, and that makes us into facilitators.' The role of facilitator is not a paradigmatic one, and therefore many people find their introduction to a therapeutic community an unnerving and confusing one (Kennard 1983), and indeed the Sisyphean problem of developing a working myth that is not based on paradigm role relationships contributes to the instability of many such communities. This is amplified by the fact that the therapeutic community tends to deny the first principle of the closed system as we have explored it so far, which is the orientation towards the even keel or the smooth running of the establishment. Whereas for most residential establishments crises are problems to be dealt with as smoothly as possible, creating minimum disruption, for the therapeutic communities they are meat and drink, and treated as opportunities for learning.

The history of therapeutic communities is littered with glorious failures – at least, failures in the sense that they did not last for very long. Homer Lane's 'Little Commonwealth' for adolescents lasted a mere three years. The special unit at Barlinnie Prison in Glasgow has been under attack since it opened, and the attack is renewed as I write. Wilfred Bion's initial tentative steps towards a therapeutic community at Northwick Park Hospital lasted a matter of weeks. The demise of the Paddington Day Hospital has been interestingly argued about in public (Baron 1984; Crockett 1985; Baron 1985).

Since people involved in such communities are as likely to succumb to splitting as anyone else, the reasons for failure are often allegedly found in the outside world rather than inside the community itself, but in this case the intolerance of the sponsoring agencies has been considerable. Therapeutic communities are often thorns in the side of conventional agencies.

TECHNICAL MYTHS

Not all myths arc based on such global assertions about human nature, of which I have chosen only the broadest in the preceding discussion. Although there are usually elements of such valuing in any myth, another significant factor is the technical model that underpins the practice rhetoric of the establishment. However, caution needs to be exercised in this area; the technical model does not translate directly into the working myth.

Behaviourism

Behaviourist theory provides one such technical model, although it does so with some difficulty because behaviourist accounts of social systems are never entirely convincing. In a description of a (fictional) community based on behaviourist principles such as Skinner's own utopia in *Walden Two* (1976), the apparent myth is one that centres on the malleability of human beings, and the role of the leaders (Skinner's community has no 'staff caste', being simply a community of 'normal' people) is that of shapers of the community members through detailed control of the environment, but without a clear value base. The book does contain a defence against the charge of fascism that is not entirely convincing, but since the behaviourist model claims to be scientific, it also claims to be value-free. Both of these claims can be contested, but they do suggest that by its own lights, behaviourism is merely a statement of means, not of ends.

More important than the technology itself, then, is the context within which it operates or the assumptions that need to be present for anyone to believe that it is appropriate to use it. For behaviourism, that context must at least be one of *change*, and in most cases one of *control*. Furthermore, explicitly behaviourally orientated units – even those that go the whole hog in the form of token economies – tend to find it difficult to apply the principles right through the constraints–procedures–reactions–interpretation cycle. The constraints of staffing ratios and time commitments often vitiate full-scale implementation of the programme, and although procedures can be devised to embody reinforcement of desirable behaviour, there remains the problem of interpretation of what constitutes such behaviour (see Buckholdt and Gubrium 1979), both at the overall programme-planning level and at the face-to-face level. The behaviourally orientated regime is aiming at a working myth which goes something like: 'We work with residents as if they were programmable machines, and that makes us technicians.' That working myth, however, does not yield very much satisfaction to the staff, and provides no support to deal with the considerable stresses of trying the apply the programme, because it is unable to account for the very unscientific feelings expressed by the residents.

Behaviourist principles are applied most frequently with mentally ill or handicapped clients, or with very disturbed young people, all of whom are groups that are difficult to empathize with. This raises the possibility of the myth that humanitarian practitioners have tried so long to avoid: 'We work with residents in here as if they were animals, and that makes us trainers.' Again, this myth is not entirely satisfactory in terms of the emotional needs of the staff (leaving aside those of the residents themselves), but it does tend to introduce the possibility of a more paradigmatic value base, which is that of seeing the co-operative client as a *pet*, with a conscientious owner – whereas the uncooperative client becomes a lion to be tamed, to use Hargreaves' analogy, or more memorably a *threat*. In either case it becomes difficult to maintain a sense of clients as 'people like us'. The formulation of a treatment contract, which is technically desirable where possible, as well as suggesting a more egalitarian relationship between the resident and the staff, may go some small way towards ameliorating this situation. In that case, we move towards the more respectful contract of: 'We work with residents in here as if they were learners, and that makes us technical resources.' This seems to me a pretty good, if slightly impersonal, working myth. However, it has to be impersonal because it is in the nature of any such technical orientation, whether behaviourist or psychoanalytic, that the staff can never step out of role. Hence it is even more difficult than in less committed establishments for any genuine reciprocal friendship to develop between residents and staff.

Depth Psychology

'Depth psychology' is a generic term that can be applied to any psychological theory that suggests that people have hidden depths, and thus includes all variants of psychoanalysis, analytical psychology, and to a certain extent the individual psychology of Alfred Adler. (In a number of important respects Adler's thinking, although not often explicitly acknowledged, provides the foundations for therapeutic community work.) Despite theoretical differences, residential establishments based on depth psychological principles are prone to three major problems at the working myth level.

The first is the inversion of the working myth, which follows when the most powerful factor in the cycle is the staff's own definition of themselves. They want to see themselves and be seen by others as a certain kind of person, and therefore they force the residents into the complementary role. Because residential work is a fairly low status occupation, some staff gain status and a degree of power by seeing themselves as psychotherapists, leading to the myth: 'We are psychotherapists and that makes the people we work with into our patients.'

The second problem is that of incompetence. This is a serious allegation to make, and I do not mean it at a general level, but the practice of depth psychotherapy is a very complex thing, training for it is rare and hard to come by, and there is no universally recognized standard qualification. People can therefore set themselves up as psychotherapists quite easily with little regulation, and while this is enough of a problem in the outside world, it is even easier to claim such expertise in the closed world of a residential establishment, where the practitioner also has a great deal of power. It is a truism in the world of counselling and psychotherapy that it is possible to get in deeper than one can cope with or contain, and in the residential establishment this can creep up on staff without their realizing it. They may therefore do more harm than good.

The third problem is the endemic *preciousness* of such establishments, by which I mean their self-absorption in the minutiae of interpretation and reinterpretation of behaviour, and their tendency to treat the outside world with contempt. This can lead to quite different standards applying within the establishment from those that apply outside, leading to problems with the 'mitigation' step on the staircase of concerns. It can also lead to a discounting and dismissal of the more mundane problems that residents have, and an unwarranted invasion of their privacy.

Both of these are fairly swingeing accusations, and there are considerations to set against them. The role of patient in psychoanalysis is for the resident a far less destructive one than that of little villain, or even pet. It suggests interesting depths, and if the resident understands (as few probably do) that the same kind of interpretation of behaviour can be applied to the staff as to himself, it does not have to suggest stigma for being a resident. Enormous commitment can be generated on the part of the staff, with an undeniable interest in every aspect of the residents' lives. And, it should be said, there are several establishments that are well aware of these dangers, and take considerable steps to overcome them, producing a working myth which is more like: 'We work with people in here as if they were struggling to overcome something they do not understand, and that makes us their gurus leading them to enlightenment.'

Most establishments espousing depth psychology ideas work with young people and some with mentally ill people. They also tend to be selective of their potential members, which is often levelled as a criticism at them, although this is not necessarily fair.

MYTHS AND THE TECHNOLOGY OF RESIDENTIAL WORK

The behaviourist and depth psychology approaches have been briefly discussed simply because they are obvious choices as technical models for some client groups. The point of doing so has not been to undermine them, but to suggest some of the transformations that can come about as attempts are made to express a theory in practice in the residential or more generally in the group setting. Both of the theories, of course, are more immediately seen as relevant to some client groups rather than others. If space permitted, a similar analysis could be undertaken of, say, religious principles in practically any sector of residential work, or the anthroposophical approach of Rudolf Steiner in work with children and adults with mental handicaps.

Most establishments, of course, are more eclectic or pragmatic in their approach. While they may be spared the problems of occasionally inappropriate dogmatism that beset more committed establishments, they also lack the reference points provided by a clear theoretical position or the committed values that provide the energy for Sisyphean change. Nevertheless, there is an increasing range of technical models at the disposal of the residential practitioner, and the myths implicit in them are worthy of study.

As suggested earlier, the problem with such models when they aspire to become working myths is that they do not provide a role for the staff member that approximates to anything that she is familiar with, and therefore managers and others who try to introduce them have to find an acceptable role for staff to take up.

Normalization

In the light of the above argument, we can return to normalization, which is an invaluable guide to the management of the mitigation step on the staircase. The difficulty with it in working myth terms is that in ordinary life there is no such thing as a staff member! One could say that if carried through fully (and if it could be carried through fully there would be no need to have such an approach – after all, truly ordinary people do not go about thinking how they can be ordinary), it would result in a myth of the order of 'We work with people in here as if they were ordinary people, and that makes us redundant!' In reality, although there is no single role of 'staff member' to help or teach ordinary people to do things, ordinary people do make use of others' assistance in a variety of capacities all the time. They give us a hand to do some physical tasks, lend us their knowledge and expertise in dealing with unfamiliar situations, offer advice and support in solving problems, and so on. So what the normalization approach as such calls for is a working myth like: 'We work with people in here as if they were ordinary people, and that makes us occasional helpers in all kinds of different ways.' The problem with using such a working myth as a slogan in the back of one's mind is that the constraints tend to belie it, and the reactions of the residents militate against it. One constraint is that staff are paid to help residents, which is not the case outside. In ordinary life, too, there is a mutuality of assistance: my neighbour and I clubbed together to hire some scaffolding for work on our houses; I helped him to put his up and then take it down and then he did the same for me. Although there is no denying that there are pay-offs from working even with difficult clients, and staff get quite a lot back for what they put into it, that is purely a bonus. It cannot be expected or relied on. The structure of 'care' (and even the very word) implies that it is the staff who do the caring and the residents who do the consuming, and there is a limit to the extent to which one can get beyond this. Alongside this is the need of the residents to find a constant basis for their relationship with the staff, and the role shifts of 'normal acquaintances' who are also 'occasional helpers' may be more complex than they can understand or adjust to. If normalization is to get beyond the stage of rhetoric and aims, therefore, it is necessary to find a relatively consistent role for the staff member to take, the nature of which will vary from setting to setting.

Reality Orientation

An associated problem besets the adoption of 24-hour reality orientation as an approach with elderly people who are confused or have dementia. To a certain extent – but only to a certain extent – the role of the staff member is a teaching one, which resembles that of the infant teacher in view of the simplicity of the ideas being taught, such as orientation to time, person, and place: 'Hello, Mrs Pickering, do you remember me? . . . What day is it today? . . . No, it's Tuesday today. What do we do on Tuesdays?' The difficulty is that such a role does not come easily when the 'pupil' is in her eighties. It sounds patronizing, even disrespectful, and in lucid periods confused old people experience it as such and may make their feelings very clear. Since it is an additional component of work rather than a replacement for anything else, staff may well be inclined to pay more lip-service to the idea than to implement it in practice. They are in need not only of a suitable model for understanding what is happening to their clients, which is a matter of knowledge, but also a form of working myth that they can internalize and which gives them a consistent role; perhaps 'We work with people in here as if they were adrift, and that makes us their link with the shore' would fill the bill.

One approach that does have a distinctive 'staff' role built into it is that of *advocacy*, as practised in work with people with a mental (or physical) handicap. (I put 'staff' in quotes, because the role of advocate may be taken by a volunteer rather than a staff member; and the potential applications are not by any means restricted to these client groups.) Unless there is an element of self-advocacy in the programme, however, it is not always clear how a working myth can construe the resident himself. Although advocacy can develop a purely dependent relationship into one that involves fighting on behalf of the client, incorporating this development into an hour-to-hour working myth requires thought, and working myths are precisely devices to avoid having to think strategies out anew in every situation.

THE 'ARTIFICIAL' MYTH

The emphasis of the discussion in the last section has shifted somewhat. Instead of looking at the working myth as a descriptive phenomenon, I have been examining ways in which approaches to residential work imported from outside, as it were, can be translated into forms that satisfy the requirements of the working myth. The challenge of change is to create the conditions under which the imported ideology does become the real working myth of the establishment in such a way that to work in accordance with it becomes second nature to the staff, and that it is correspondingly accepted by the residents themselves. It should not be forgotten that they too have their part to play in the formation of the working myth, although it is only the 'reactions' phase of the myth creation cycle to which they contribute directly, which is of course a reflection of the power relationships within the establishment. The danger of change is always that of distortion or transformation of the rhetoric or aims as the cycle of myth formation proceeds.

Two considerations come into play at this point. The first is that of judging the *appropriateness or otherwise of a particular myth to a particular task*. Although some of the myths that have been sketched in may be found objectionable on ethical grounds, the most common problems stem from the lack of 'fit' between the working myth and the task of the establishment. Up to now the notion of task has been somewhat neglected, because the focus of the discussion has been on the proceedings within the four walls of the establishment, without reference to what it is actually intended to do in relation to the outside world. That world is both where the power is located to demand that the establishment perform in a certain way, and the world of potential and former clients of the establishment. Indeed, task performance is not *necessarily* mentioned at all in the cycle of myth formation, although it may be implicit in the rhetoric or the statement of aims. Task considerations need to take into account transactions across the boundary of the establishment, which will be considered in Chapter 9.

The second consideration is that *ensuring the adoption of a particular working myth is only possible if there is an acceptable role for the staff members*. Acceptability, in this context, refers both to their willingness to take on the role (if you get 'Oh, I can't see myself doing *that*', you have problems) and the practicability of their assuming it. It may be, as the staircase model points out, that there is just no time to act in the way that is implied, or it may be that the role demanded by the myth is beyond the competence of the present staff because of their lack of experience or training. If the role is not acceptable, then another working myth will evolve, which implies a role that *is* acceptable to them.

THE FAMILY MYTH

I have left until last consideration of the most powerful basis for the constitution of working myths, which is the ultimate paradigm case of the family. Davis (1981) has pointed out the extent to which residential establishments can be defined with reference to the family, and that this is the reference point by which their performance is frequently judged. Thus she identifies establishments that function as *family alternatives*, *family substitutes*, or *family complements*. There are basically two reasons for the potency of the family myth. The first is the experience of the family as the basic unit of care that the majority of us share, and the consequent tendency to relate back all other experiences of looking after others to that most powerful paradigm, which is ultimately the mother–child bond and relationship. The second is the fact that the family is the 'default' institution, the one that gets the job of looking after dependent people if no one else takes it on.

Family group homes for children, which have largely been superseded by placing all but the most difficult child clients in foster-care (which is of course even closer as a model to the natural family than any institution), often used to adopt the family working myth to quite good effect. Children were aware that the housemother and her husband, 'pursuing his own occupation' in the words of the job advertisements, were not their *real* family, but the closeness was emphasized by encouraging them to call the staff not 'Mum' and 'Dad', but 'Aunty' and 'Uncle'. In the best examples, the continuity of care and the closeness of the small group were such that the myth could be sustained quite well by all concerned. As social work thinking developed, however, it became less and less appropriate. It was felt that for a child to spend his or her entire childhood in such a setting was not desirable, and as efforts to reunite natural families were pursued, the family myth of the group home became as much a liability as an asset. Moreover, the experience of many adolescents growing up in such establishments was that the pseudo-family was less capable of acting as a container for their adolescent acting-out than was an ideal real family, and so they suffered the cruel fate of being rejected from a group in which they had placed a great personal investment.

Nevertheless, the family myth is one that has great appeal for many new entrants to residential work with young people, often expressed by young staff in terms of being a 'big sister' or 'elder brother' to the clients. It is of course more difficult to apply so directly to work with adult or elderly clients, but it is no accident that there is a tendency to refer to clients with a mental handicap as being like children (thereby giving scope for a family-based paradigm role for staff), or for some staff in old people's homes to address residents as 'Gran'.

It is precisely the potency and paradigmatic nature of the family myth that makes it so difficult to evaluate, in terms of its contribution to or distraction from task performance. Davis' categories form a useful starting point, but it is also necessary to develop other ways of looking at the dependent relationship as it is expressed in residential settings before one can get sufficiently beyond primitive feelings about the family to make informed judgements. One alternative way of looking at this almost universal dependent component of residential theory and practice is put forward in the next chapter.

8 Of Skeletons and Shells

Whatever the working myth of the establishment, one can be pretty sure that one component of it will include a position on the Skeleton–Shell continuum, and a covert policy on handling variations from this preferred position. This continuum is a construct, or model, which relates the internal features of a residential establishment to the external demands on it, and to psychological factors in the experience of the residents. Working myths that emphasize the capabilities of residents will be towards the Skeleton end, and those that dwell on their disabilities will be towards the Shell end.

The terms 'Skeleton' and 'Shell' indicate that it is based on an analogy, in this case with zoology. By relating factors in the context and the internal life of residential establishments to the opposed principles of Skeleton and Shell, the aim is to arrive at a useful – although by no means exhaustive – account of what goes on in an establishment. This account is descriptive, not prescriptive. What one chooses to make of it in practice will depend a great deal on the kind of establishment with which one is concerned, the needs of the residents, and the pressures from outside.

The basic elements of the model are set out in this chapter as a series of propositions as follows:

1. *The Skeleton and the Shell represent two fundamentally different ways of structuring bodies in the animal kingdom.* Every multicelled animal above the most primitive level requires some means of maintaining its shape, and of enabling it to interact in its particular fashion with the outside world. Biologists make the basic distinction between *vertebrate* and *invertebrate* animals; for present purposes we shall distort this a little and refer to skeleton-based and shell-based animals. (In the discussion that follows, 'skeleton' and 'shell' will refer to biological features, and Skeleton and Shell, capitalized, will

refer to the construct derived from them.) The skeleton is the kind of structure in which the organs of the body are, as it were, hung around an internal framework; the shell is the alternative structure in which they are packed into a box.

Skeleton and shell structures are rarely found in their pure form in nature. Some higher animals, such as turtles and armadillos, appear to have both (although the shell is primarily a means of protection for them, rather than the basis of their anatomical structure). Practically all animals with skeletons also have a skull, which may be seen as a shell for the brain. The construct is an idealized one, to represent two different principles, and it is merely an analogy. The fact that it is not pure in nature serves as a reminder that it can never be a pure distinction as an analogy, either – and indeed as it goes on, the argument of the paper will take us further and further from the original basis.

For the moment, we can make basic distinctions between the qualities of the two; as listed in Table 8.1.

Table 8.1 Basic distinctions between skeleton and shell structures

Skeleton	Shell
Internal	External
Supports	Contains
the two structures in themselves leave the animal:	
Vulnerable	Protected
the structures are:	
Flexible	Rigid
and make growth and adaptation*:	
Easy	Difficult

* On this latter point, consider that when a skeleton-based animal grows, all that it has to do is grow the bones, and the skin stretches around them, but that the process of growth for a shell-based animal is much more complicated. Crabs, for example, have to grow new shells folded up inside their old ones, then shed the old ones, and remain very vulnerable for some hours while they 'inflate' the new one to its full size and let it harden.

2. *The Skeleton and the Shell represent two fundamentally different tendencies in social relations.* The notion of two fundamentally opposed tendencies underlying the universe is very ancient. In western thinking such dichotomies have usually been underpinned by the assumption that one side was 'good' and the other 'bad'. In the east, it has been recognized that both might well be necessary, and that one is not to be preferred to the other; the major example is the Chinese construct of Yin and Yang. It must be emphasized that apart from our cultural preconceptions, in this model *neither Skeleton nor Shell is 'better' than the other*.

There is a temptation to reduce Skeleton and Shell to the distinction between 'individuality' and 'corporateness', or between 'independence' and 'dependence', which are relatively familiar. Such distinctions are important parts of the Skeleton/ Shell construct, but by no means are they the whole story. At root the distinction is about assumptions about human nature, and which 'side' of that nature takes priority. It is reflected in political philosophies, in differing theologies (sometimes coexisting uneasily within the same religion), in cultures, and in personal relations.

The Skeleton view holds that people are normally expected to live on the basis of their own *internal* resources, contained within their own bodies. People are believed to find the basis of their selfhood and their value inside themselves, and to be obliged to create the structure for their lives from within.

The Shell view suggests that the individual can only find a meaningful structure for life with reference to something *external*, and that there is no adequate basis internally on which to base rules, judgements, or performance.

3. *It is the general assumption in our society that people will survive on the basis of their personal Skeletons.* This simply means that we assume that people carry sufficient structure around inside themselves to enable them to live and work together with others. This is not a great philosophical notion – on the contrary, parts of it are very simple, basic, and practical. People are expected to have certain physical skills (and associated sensory competence) such as being able to walk

around, pick things up and handle them, make tea, dress themselves, and so on. They are also expected to have a basically adequate intellectual structure, which enables them to read and write, fill in forms, and pay for things in shops, and a different kind of mental structure in the form of a degree of emotional control, so that their feelings do not get too much in the way of their ordinary practical activities, and they can sustain relationships. Finally, although most problematic and difficult to discuss, they need some kind of moral structure, which enables them to live with their fellows without hurting or exploiting them and their property more than the dominant ideology of their society allows them to. This list offers no more than the merest pointers to the basic achievements required to be a fully paid-up member of our society, but it can be seen that such requirements are very mundane. At such a level, of course, all societies have similar requirements; the difference tends to come in their assumptions about the nature of personal identity.

Some people cannot manage on their own, however; their physical, intellectual, emotional, or moral Skeletons are not strong enough. The analogy is recognized in common speech when we talk about people who lack 'backbone' or 'moral fibre' or 'need to stand on their own two feet'. There are those whose physical structure is not up to the requirements of daily life (and I am not restricting myself to orthopaedic disabilities here), either because of short-term illnesses or chronic disabilities including sensory impairment. There are those whose intellectual Skeletons are inadequate. There are those whose emotional Skeletons cannot cope – they suffer mental distress to the extent that normal life is beyond them, sometimes in their own eyes and sometimes in the eyes of those who live with them. And there are children, who are believed in our society not yet to have developed sufficient Skeleton of their own to be able to survive 'independently'.

4. *It is also the general assumption that living in a Shell structure is a response to Skeleton failure*. Going back to bodily structure for a moment: if you break a limb, the treatment is

for it to be put in splints or a plaster cast. Effectively, this means that skeleton failure is responded to by the provision of a temporary shell, which takes the strain and pressure off the bone while it knits together again. If the plaster is left on too long, the muscles of the limb atrophy, and even the bone itself may weaken through not having enough work to do, so that the internal structure is rendered less effective than it was before. In the case of chronic failure of the bodily structure, the shell may have to be permanent (*e.g.*, although it relates to the failure of muscles and control rather than bones, using a caliper to enable a polio victim to walk).

In the same way, we respond to the needs of those who are incapable of managing on the basis of their Skeletons by providing them with a Shell – a protective institution that limits the demands made on them, and caters for the needs they are unable to satisfy for themselves. The most 'normal' example of this is the family: children are cared for in families where food and shelter are provided without having to be earned, and where control and oversight are exercised over them until such time as they are grown and socialized enough to be thought capable of going their own way. It is important that the family is so organized that the child can dispose of it when it becomes appropriate to do so. Failure to enable grown children to move out of the family setting – which can cause considerable pain to the parents – keeps them unduly dependent and unable to look after themselves, just like keeping the plaster on for too long.

The same system applies in the case of those who are socially disabled. In the event that they are not capable of living 'in the community' (whatever that means), they are admitted to institutions that are designed to function as Shells (see Table 8.2). A list of such forms of Skeleton failure and the Shell responses throws up a number of issues for social policy.

First there is the question of the suitability of the Shell to the needs of the individual (and even the category of Skeleton failure to which they belong). In the category 'physical competence', for example, it is clear that mere inability to walk, or deafness, does not constitute total disqualification from

Table 8.2 Reasons for provision of social Shell

Skeleton requirement	Skeleton failure	Social Shell
Less problematic		
Overall maturity	Youth	Family, school
Physical competence	Physical illness or disability	Hospital, family or hostel
Intellectual competence	Mental handicap	Hospital, school, family, hostel, group home, social education centre, etc.
Emotional competence	Mental disturbance	Hospital, family, hostel, drugs
Moral competence	Delinquency	Supervision . . . . . . prison
More problematic		

ordinary Skeleton functioning in a wide variety of activities. Total paralysis or deafness combined with visual impairment, on the other hand, may well exclude people from normal functioning on a much wider front. The difficulty of providing a suitable range of Shell facilities is not only a practical one in that most of them are group-based and therefore have to be designed for categories of people rather than individuals, but is also a matter of prejudice on the part of the wider community. Providing a Shell is no longer seen, at least by the professionals involved, in terms of putting people away so that they are 'out of sight and out of mind'; but among other factors the Skeleton feature of accountability comes in to demand that risk be minimized. The outcome is that all too often a Shell is provided that is far too complete to compensate for the Skeleton deficiency (Wagner 1988). The prime example of a social Shell is residential care; and institutionalization is the social equivalent of the atrophy of the Skeleton as a result of too complete a Shell.

Second, there is the problem of defining Skeleton failure. As the table indicates, there is relatively little argument in our culture as to the need for a Shell to protect and care for children. Indeed, for a long time the family has been seen as the paradigm (often the only paradigm) for social Shells (Davis 1981). Even here there is a problem: at what age, or by what criteria, does one accept that the Skeleton is strong enough to sustain an 'independent' existence, and particularly independent choice? Our culture's extended limbo of adolescence points to confusion over the issue. For physically handicapped people, there is little argument about their need for Shell provision of some kind; but there is argument about its extent (see above and Miller and Gwynne's view of being in residential care as 'social death', 1972).

For people with a mental handicap, the issue is getting rather more difficult. The child acknowledges his need for the family, at least until adolescence. The person with a physical handicap also knows that he needs some assistance. The person with a mental handicap may not know that, although his lack of understanding may be a function of his overall problem. However, even if the authority is conceded to others to make the decision about the need for a Shell, in many cases there is confusion about the criteria to be used to make judgements about it. Judgements about the adequacy of intellectual functioning are relative to the requirements of the society at large – the acceptable level may be much lower in peasant communities than in technological ones, for example. More difficult still are the questions surrounding those forms of emotional (and cognitive) and moral incapacity that are deemed to be in need of a Shell response. The debate about the nature of mental illness is only part of the issue; it extends further into the morality and effectiveness of imposed treatment. The notion of 'treatment' itself is a Shell one: the recipient is a 'patient', and the responsibility for what is done to the patient is seen to be taken by the doctor (Brickman *et al.* 1982). For mental patients, the Shell may not be residential provision within a hospital, but the use of psychotropic drugs that have a containing effect in their sedative potential as well as their other effects.

When we get to the area of moral failure, the philosophical issues become even more complex. Moral failure is defined by convention (*i.e.* law), and its definers are in an adversarial relationship with the offender. While justice and the protection of innocent citizens are clearly requirements of the state, the forms of law may well be reflections of vested interests among the powers that be as much as of the consensus of citizens. Whether the response to offences should be at the level of retribution or treatment is a similarly fraught question.

As the questions about the nature of Skeleton failure become more complex, so the variety of Shell responses becomes greater, and the part played by the political and judicial systems in decision-making grows larger.

Despite there being more old people in care in this country than any other single group, they do not appear as a separate category within Table 8.2. Their Skeleton failure, if any, is to be found in any of the other categories – we have not yet reached the stage where merely being old is a sufficient basis for providing an automatic Shell structure.

The potency of the Shell structure provided for an individual should depend on the extent of Skeleton failure, but falling into more than one category has a tendency to reinforce the social demand for a complete Shell. This accounts in some measure for the extremity of the response to moral failure among young people. The Approved School and later CH(E) system persisted far after its ineffectiveness was demonstrated in the case of the many of the young people in it, and the gut response is still that a 'short sharp shock' *must* be effective.

The moral of this perfunctory survey would seem at first sight to be that Shells should be kept as weak as possible, and that Skeleton autonomy should be preserved as far as possible. However, the issue is not quite that simple. As we saw in the discussion of the 'warehousing' and 'horticultural' myths, some people have problems (such as degenerative physical disorders, or the compounding effects of increasing age), which mean that their Shell requirements will become greater rather than less. And, as the second part of this chapter will show, paradoxically the provision of an adequate Shell structure is necessary to

Table 8.3 *Pattern of relatedness: individual to group*

Skeleton	Shell
relating to choices:	
Individual free to choose	Choices made for one
to control:	
Self-control	External control
hence:	
Individual responsible for actions	Not responsible for actions
which leads to emphasis on:	
Individuality	Corporateness

permit optimum Skeleton functioning.

5. *The natural tendency of a residential establishment is in the direction of increased Shell structuring.* We now turn to the residential setting itself, with an elaboration of the features of the Skeleton and the Shell modes (Table 8.3). To recap for a moment: I argued in Chapter 3 that a residential establishment can be usefully regarded as a self-regulating social system, with its own feedback devices, which enable it to maintain a steady state in the face of efforts to change it. I also argued that the natural tendency of such a system in the case of a residential establishment is to 'sink to' the level of 'administrative convenience' in its internal policies and practices (*i.e.* that administrative convenience is the equilibrium state of the system), and that any attempt to operate on any other basis is ultimately the product of the values and commitments, rather than the knowledge or the skills, of the staff group (Chapter 5).

I now wish to go further, and to suggest that administrative convenience is largely synonymous with the maintenance of the Shell mode. The reasons are not hard to find, within Table 8.3. The management of large groups of people, all wanting to make choices for themselves, is difficult. It is very demanding to concede such autonomy to individuals within any residential setting; the few places that do manage it tend to be very expensive hotels. Practicable cleaning arrangements tend to dictate when people have to be out of bed; cooking arrangements govern mealtimes; if menu choice is practical, it can rarely allow for spontaneous changes of mind without waste, and so on. Consultation procedures over changes that may effect residents' lives are cumbersome and time-consuming. Unless strongly held convictions demand otherwise, it is a lot simpler to deal with routine aspects of the life of the establishment as if residents were a homogeneous group, and on the whole they do not protest very much. (If they do protest, of course, the system ceases to be administratively convenient, and on the whole a more Skeleton-orientated working myth evolves.) Corporate treatment of residents, and the assumption of much decision-making by the senior staff, easily become the stock-in-trade of most establishments. This in its turn is made much easier if it is accompanied by the ideology that maintains that residents are unwilling or incapable of making many choices for themselves, and conformity to the procedures of the establishment becomes the criterion for the assessment of a 'good' or co-operative resident, which naturally means that external control of the residents assumes more importance than their own internal self-control. Indeed, that self-control, with its implied capacity for making personal decisions and choices, can easily become an undesirable trait.

This sequence of the creation of dependence is self-reinforcing the less capable residents are of making choices for themselves, the more homogeneous the group becomes, and the more easily it can be managed.

The process is largely an internal one, but it needs also to be seen in the context of the residential establishment as a Shell structure. Social expectations which have already been alluded to, such as those of the reduction of risk in the care of those who need Shells, tend to reinforce the process from outside. The net result is that the Skeleton attributes of the residents tend to be devalued and even to be sanctioned against. 'Looping' also takes place – the reinterpretation of the behaviour of residents in the light of the assumptions of the establishment. Protests and conflict about routines and procedures that would in the outside world have been treated as arguments about reality are reinterpreted as further evidence of the pathology of the resident, and indeed the lack of opportunity for the expression of such protests often leads to displaced protest behaviour, which is very easy to reinterpret in such a way. The mentally handicapped resident who throws his dinner at the staff in frustration is rarely seen as making a valid comment about the quality of the food or his personal tastes (see below on 'catastrophic oscillation').

Further features of such Skeleton and Shell structures now become apparent in the light of this argument (Table 8.4). The hard-to-manage/easy-to-manage construct has already been explored, but it does have one other dimension: *that the staff themselves are the prisoners of the Shell structure as much as the residents*. 'Prisoners' may be too dramatic a word, but the pressures of the job are such that staff too seek ways of avoiding total reliance on their personal Skeletons, and find them in the structuring and routinization of life in the establishment. Like the residents, the more established this becomes, the less they are able to think in alternative terms. It is only when staff can be provided with alternative constructive ways of meeting Shell needs, in the form of supervision or other means of staff support and development, that they do not have to seek them in the institutionalization of the regime.

Table 8.4 Internal features of culture of Skeleton and Shell Communities

Skeleton	Shell
Characteristics of social structures:	
Hard to manage Guilt-culture	Easy to manage Shame-culture
with associated ways of thinking:	
Scientific (reality-based)	Magical, symbolic (fantasy-based)

While shame-culture is not confined to Shell structures, it does tend to flourish there. In a guilt-culture the individual who has offended feels *guilty* for what he has done, whether or not anyone else knows about it. He does not feel guilty if he knows that he has not done it, even if everyone else believes that he has. In shame-culture the offender's response is shame if other people believe that he has committed the offence, regardless of whether or not he did so. If they do not find out about it, he feels nothing. From the point of view of other people in shame-culture, the important thing is the individual's apparent *involvement in* the offence, regardless of his moral responsibility for it. Such shame-culture thinking appears to be endemic in residential establishments, among both residents and staff (Atherton 1983; Benedict 1967).

Shame-culture can easily be identified with magical thinking, in which resemblance and metonymy dominate in establishing connections between events and individuals, rather than scientific thinking, in which hypotheses are put to the test and falsified (albeit within the framework of the prevalent paradigm). The potency of such fantasy is dangerous when staff are in the business of making judgements that affect the course of individuals' lives (Atherton 1982).

Both the above elements are suggestive of a generally regressed way of thinking that prevails in many establishments, and is consistent with the high degree of dependence engendered, which may well exceed what is necessary at a physical or controlling level in order to provide an appropriate Shell for the needs of the residents.

6. *Both Skeleton and Shell elements are necessary for a normal life.* So far, the features of the Shell have come out of this discussion rather badly, and indeed our cultural bias is such as to emphasize the virtues of the Skeleton. These are the famous Victorian virtues of self-help and self-reliance that are currently being extolled more than ever (and seem to be characteristic of the 1980s, not only in Britain). However, I have been looking at the *inappropriate* use of the Shell as I have discussed judgements made about the need for residential care,

and the internal life of the institutionalized establishment. In some other, mainly eastern, cultures the Shell side of things is valued more than the Skeleton side. Indeed, it can be maintained that it is the west that is deviant in its Skeleton emphasis; so the Shell is only a 'bad thing' when it is misused and misapplied.

In this part of the discussion I wish to correct the balance by suggesting that both Skeleton *and* Shell have their parts to play, and need to be incorporated in the life of the establishment. I hope that by now the reader has got the general 'feel' of the construct, because we now move further away from the original biological analogy.

All of us need a Shell some of the time, and most of us work in our Skeleton most of the time. Autonomy and facing new challenges are important if we are to learn, make progress, develop, and make relationships. They are essential in most of the things that we take for granted as being 'good' features of a human being reaching his or her full potential as understood in our society. But we cannot exercise our autonomy unless we have some basis of security from which to start; and we have to keep returning to that base (or that Shell) in order to reassure ourselves (see Reed (1978) for a similar view with different terminology).

A similar pattern can be detected in many areas of psychological investigation. Learning curves show periods of progression and periods of consolidation. Studies of young children remind us how they alternate between being venturesome and seeking stimulation, and returning to their mothers for reassurance. Stages of transition in life are accompanied by predictable rituals. Maslow (1987) and Erikson (1965), in their models of human needs and development respectively, point out the necessity of going back and recapitulating what has already been achieved. Anthropologists have identified similar processes in whole communities – periods of getting things done alternating with occasions of getting together to re-cement the 'togetherness' of the group. Many organisations show similar features. 'Progress' is not a straight line – it is a complex curve of peaks and troughs –

Table 8.5 Psychological features of Skeleton and Shell

Skeleton	Shell
Stress	Relaxation
Risk	Security
Unfamiliarity	Predictability
Conflict	Accommodation
(Growth)	(Regression)

although I choose to represent it as a side-to-side rather than up-and-down movement because I want to encourage a neutral evaluation of Skeleton and Shell.

We can now summarize some further features of Skeleton and Shell that are suggested by the above observations (Table 8.5).

Before we take this analysis further, a word is in order about the terminology used in Table 8.5. Stress is not necessarily a bad thing. Some writers distinguish between necessary stress, which is the 'spice of life', and *dis*tress, which is what happens when stress gets to be too much (Selye 1974). Unfamiliarity seems at first sight to be a fairly 'weak' feature to choose to characterize Skeleton activity, but its potency can be seen in the case of culture shock and similar experiences of disorientation (Furnham and Bochner 1986). The opposite of 'conflict' is generally taken to be 'co-operation', but we are talking constructs here, not dictionary opposites. 'Accommodation' is used in the sense of 'going along with things', that is, allowing one's life to be structured by external factors. Co-operation can in fact involve quite a lot of stress and risk. 'Regression', as used here, does not *necessarily* imply the defence mechanism of reverting to old and familiar ways of doing things, but does embrace that. It is a broader usage of the term to suggest the movement towards consolidation, and necessary retreat to recuperate ('retire and re-group' in military terminology).

All of the above are *psychological* states. They may or may not be appropriate to the prevailing circumstances, and different people will experience them for different reasons and in different ways. It is very much a case of 'one man's meat is another man's poison'. At the psychological level one person's Skeleton is another person's Shell, although there are Shell experiences that are common to many people. For one person, going for a long walk in the hills may be relaxation, and a chance to unwind from a stressful daily round. For another the same activity may be seen as risky (we might get lost), stressful (mainly in a physical sense), but also possibly an occasion for growth (an assumption behind adventure training). For both, a drink in a country pub at the end of the walk, however, may well have strong Shell elements. Even the same activity can have different significance for the same person on different occasions. There is nothing that I enjoy more than a good abstruse intellectual argument with friends at a dinner party, with nothing riding on the outcome. The atmosphere makes that into a Shell activity; but a similar argument at work is very much Skeleton. The people with whom I am arguing may very well experience the whole thing quite differently.

Personal evaluation of whether it is 'better' to be in Skeleton or in Shell also varies according to where one is in the oscillation cycle. The opposite pole tends to be seen negatively while it is being moved away from, and until such time as the person is ready to move back into it. This has important implications for the timing of interventions, as will become apparent later (see the remarks on synchronization, p. 173). It also accounts for common phenomena of ambivalence about the prospect of, for example, a challenging activity. The prospect of leaving care, from a predominantly Shell-based structure to a greater reliance on Skeleton, is a case in point. At certain times it is welcomed because of the freedom and 'independence' it is assumed to afford; at other times it is a fearful prospect. Since cultural factors militate against the expression of the fears and anxieties and the suppressed or even repressed desire to retain the Shell, these tend to be expressed in deviant ways. There is clearly a need to respect the Shell elements sufficiently to permit their expression, and for the provision of a good enough Shell base to maximize Skeleton functioning – a consideration that is often sorely neglected with the consequence of failed rehabilitation.

In other words, at this level Skeleton and Shell are defined phenomenologically. In practical terms, however, this need not make that much difference, because people who define central events in daily living as embodying the opposite pole to that experienced by the majority are fairly rare birds, although it must be admitted that the *strength* with which a given activity embodies Shell or Skeleton may vary a lot. For most people, mealtimes and bed are primarily Shell, which is an important consideration in the residential setting. Baths and sex, however, are probably experienced in widely differing ways, some of which have little or nothing to do with Skeleton or Shell. I suspect, although I cannot demonstrate it without resort to unwarranted stereotyping, that women and men may differ significantly in their attribution of circumstances to Skeleton and Shell.

7. *Everyone – client and staff, strong and weak, old and young – oscillates between Skeleton and Shell.* In the light of preceding discussion, this general principle should be clear. What remains to be elaborated, however, is the different ways in which such oscillation takes place. The following diagrams attempt to represent graphically the common forms of oscillation. It should be noted that the vertical line separating the Skeleton 'zone' from the Shell 'zone' is merely a graphic convention, and that there is no such clear boundary in the real world; and that while the limits of Skeleton and Shell represent the socially constructed forms that they take, the important consideration for the individual is the extent of *movement* between his or her *personal* poles, not the 'absolute' extent to which he or she penetrates into the Skeleton or Shell zones.

Figure 8.1 shows the form taken by the oscillation in the life of a so-called 'normal' person, if such an animal exists. In our culture more time is spent in Skeleton than in Shell (which fits with the earlier assumptions of the model), and hence a little Shell goes quite a long way in facilitating continued Skeleton performance.

Figure 8.2 shows the pattern of a similarly idealised client of residential services. Whereas most of the oscillation takes place

Figure 8.1 Pattern of oscillation of 'normal' person

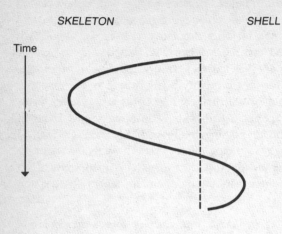

SKELETON   SHELL

Time

Figure 8.2 Pattern of oscillation of 'typical' resident

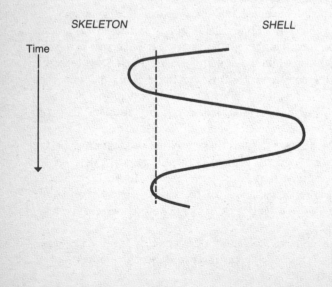

SKELETON   SHELL

Time

Figure 8.3 Common-sense view of the nature of progress of a client

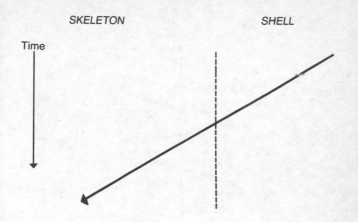

on the Shell side of the arbitrary threshold line, the movement between the most Skeleton pole and the most Shell pole is for this individual of similar magnitude to that of Figure 8.1.

Set alongside this, we need to note the common assumption about what constitutes 'progress' on the part of a client. This seems to be the view that there is a straight-line movement from the permanent Shell state to the permanent Skeleton state, one effect of which is to regard any regression as a form of relapse (Fig. 8.3).

As Figure 8.4 shows, it is more realistic to recognize that regression is a normal part not only of progress, but also of life in general, and therefore to be prepared for apparent backward steps that are in fact integral parts of the generally Skeleton-ward movement of the client. To expect a client to progress tirelessly towards his or her goal without any opportunity to recuperate or to consolidate is to expect more of him or her than of oneself.

As with any wave form, the Skeleton–Shell oscillation is subject to variation in both period (the length of time taken to

Figure 8.4 More realistic view of progress

move from one pole or peak of a wave to another) and amplitude (or pitch; the distance from a positive peak to a negative one).

Figure 8.5 shows a situation in which an individual (whether in residential provision or not – the whole wave form can be moved further to the right to represent the case of the client) cannot afford to go very far into Skeleton precisely because he is not able to go very far into Shell. If the roots do not go very deep, the plant cannot safely grow very tall, to change the biological analogy. Two things are worthy of note in this case: first, it points to the need for Shell support in order to facilitate Skeleton activity, and second, it points to the problem of individual variations. In social work it is not uncommon to come across people who seem to belie this pattern. It seems that despite having been deprived of the most basic psychological security in childhood, or even in the present, they nevertheless venture forth quite happily – if sometimes irresponsibly in the eyes of conventional society – and take great risks to survive in a very insecure world. However, for some of these people what would

Figure 8.5 Insecurity

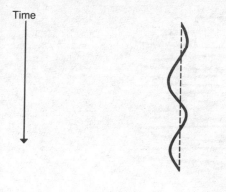

SKELETON   SHELL

Time

appear to be Skeleton activity for most of us is a kind of Shell for them, often because of its sheer familiarity and predictability; and for some there is a kind of unacknowledged desire to fail in Skeleton activity, so that society will respond by providing a Shell (a not unfamiliar pattern in the case of recidivists, and particularly those who prove to be 'untrustworthy' when tried with non-custodial sentences). The paradoxical result of this analysis is to suggest that the most effective intervention for people caught in this pattern may be the provision of voluntary Shell structures.

Occasionally one encounters exceptional individuals who seem to be able to go out on a Skeleton limb in a healthy way for an enormous length of time, and seem to lack any visible means of Shell support. Although there may be several reasons for this – and the invisibility of the Shell support to an outsider does not mean that it does not exist for the person herself – it may have some basis in a 'spiritual' Shell. For better or for worse, whether one is speaking of a saint or a terrorist, the conviction that ultimate security is to be found through a

Figure 8.6 Ephemeral oscillation

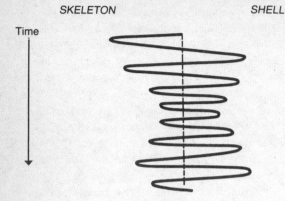

religious faith enables people to tolerate enormous uncertainty in other aspects of their lives, although the Church as we understand it is not very good at recognizing its role in providing this kind of Shell (Reed 1978).

The period of oscillation – in terms of how long one can spend in either Skeleton or Shell – is therefore also an important variable governing conduct in the world. Although the period is very variable among 'normal' people (and indeed may show patterns of mini-oscillations within major periods), extending from a matter of a day to several weeks, there is a distinct deviant form that may be termed 'ephemeral oscillation' (Fig. 8.6).

Ephemeral oscillation is normal among young children, whose time spent in Skeleton may be of the order of only a few minutes at once, and who then need to be reassured by a brief retreat into Shell before venturing forth again to explore. The period of oscillation gradually grows with the person, however, and to find ephemeral oscillation in the adult may fairly be typified as deviant. It can be extremely disabling, as well as frustrating for those who have to work with people who have such a pattern. They are seemingly perpetually seeking reassurance and support, and yet never stay long enough in Shell for one to feel that one has been able to achieve anything with them. The continual demand for attention may also lead a helper to discount the reality of their Skeleton activity, and to see them as more dependent than they actually are. It may be that this pattern relates to what has been termed 'learned helplessness' (Seligman 1974).

Examining periods of oscillation leads on to a practical issue within residential provision. It is desirable for the daily routine of the residential establishment to provide as much as possible for the oscillation of the residents, even though they may not go very far into Skeleton as conventionally understood. The familiar punctuation marks of the day – mealtimes, getting up and going to bed, and similar ritual or at least routine activities peculiar to each establishment – are commonly used on an intuitive basis to provide explicit Shell support. There may even be longer-term cycles as well. This is fine as long as the residents are capable of synchronizing with the corporate oscillation of the establishment. Some of them, however, may be out of step, or in Thoreau's phrase, 'marching to a different drummer'. Recognition of this possibility makes sense of periodic bouts of uncooperativeness on the part of residents who are equally periodically quite in tune with the life of the establishment. Explanations are normally sought in terms of individual pathology or of external events, while the most potent factor may be found in the gradual movement of the resident (or the staff member) in and out of synchrony with the rest of the establishment.

The assumption behind Figure 8.7, of course, is that the establishment does manage its own oscillation effectively, in such a way as to facilitate the oscillation of most of its members. Regrettably, this is not always the case. There are still residential establishments that conform to the pattern of the first part of this chapter, providing an unremitting Shell environment for their residents. This failure to acknowledge a normal cycle tends to lead to 'catastrophic oscillation', which is

Figure 8.7 Lack of synchronization between resident and establishment

SKELETON   SHELL

Time

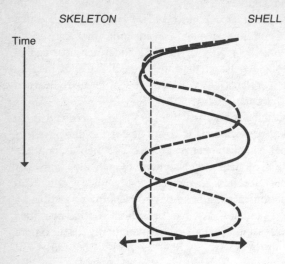

(Dotted line represents resident; solid line, establishment)

characterized by uncontrolled swings by the residents and the staff from one peak to another, in a manner that is usually fairly destructive for all concerned (Fig. 8.8). The only form of Skeleton expression that is available is conflict, for two reasons. First, any attempt to get away from the smothering Shell structure is seen as conflict by the staff, and therefore made into the occasion for a fight; and second, the only way in which residents can express their Skeletons is by setting up a conflict, which is by definition a Skeleton activity. The conflict may be with staff, or it may be within the resident group as a form of subcultural expression. In either case it tends to persist until the need to express the Skeleton side has been played out, whereupon the staff reassert their power, and probably exacerbate the next round by increasing the oppressive element of the Shell environment.

Figure 8.8 Catastrophic oscillation

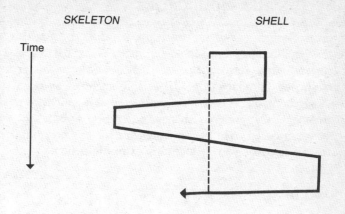

A variation on this form is to be found in some avowedly 'liberal' (or 'horticultural') residential establishments, in which the starting point is a continual insistence on the part of the powers-that-be that residents spend all their time in Skeleton, at least to a degree that is greater than they can tolerate. The response then is to exploit the Skeleton activity to an extent that goes beyond the tolerance of the staff group, such that they are forced to impose more structure and hence create the Shell environment. However, since neither the staff nor the residents are comfortable with this, the Shell culture is likely to be imposed covertly, and there is indeed a danger of setting up a double-bind in which no one knows where they stand because of the double messages, and it is impossible to engage in constructive dialogue to change the situation.

9 Across the Boundaries

So far this book has largely been about processes that determine what happens *inside* residential establishments, in spite of the reference in the Introduction to the establishment as an open system, suggesting that it cannot be considered in isolation from its environment. The previous chapter touched on some of the pressures experienced from the environment, but it is now time to widen the discussion to include this extra dimension.

BOUNDARIES

In the light of the discussion so far, we can re-examine the notion of boundaries begun in Chapter 1. A boundary is the point at which one system finishes and another begins. It is a complex notion to spell out, but relatively easy to recognize in practical terms. The complexity stems not only from the fact that systems can be nested inside, overlap, or lie alongside each other, but also from the way in which the definition of boundaries depends on the frame of reference one is using, as indeed does the definition of a 'system'. This is certainly a major problem in social work, as we have seen in the case of Mrs Jones.

In a sense, residential social work has suffered from the fact that it has *not* experienced boundaries as a problem. The boundaries are simply too obvious – they are effectively the four walls of the building itself. Until recently, and even now with some client groups, there has been no contact with potential residents before their admission, and no follow-up after their departure. Important though what happens inside the establishment may be (and if I did not think it important I would not have devoted most of this book to it) it is all too easy for the residential practitioner to forget the context within which she works. Once the question of boundaries is raised as a live issue, we are presented with a number of problems that call into question the very existence of residential provision, an existence that should indeed be questioned.

Finding the Right System

First, there is the question of whether one is intervening in the right system, defined by the most useful boundaries. Removal of the main target of intervention to live somewhere else is often the simplest solution to a problem in the short term, but may store up further problems for the long term. Removal of a family member to a mental hospital (or any other residential setting) can lead to 'closure' (Scott and Starr 1981). Admission makes them into a new kind of being, a 'psychiatric patient', or more crudely an officially recognized mad person, and hence a *non-person*. This increases the likelihood of the patients being scapegoated for the problems of the family system, and makes him or her into less than a member of the family – so that it is almost impossible for him or her to return with the same status as before. Admission buys into fantasies and myths about madness and the mad person as someone completely alien. The crisis intervention approach pioneered by Scott and his colleagues therefore insists on focusing on the family unit as both the client and the target of intervention, and on enabling the family to continue to function by recognizing that the crisis that precipitates the demand for admission is something to which all of them have contributed and with which they all need help and not blame – that the mother's exhaustion is the precipitating event as much as the bizarre behaviour of the son. Without necessarily going all the way with theorists who talk about the schizophrenic family as a whole, this approach suggests that all the family have a problem, and thereby shifts the boundary of the problem from something that is happening inside the potential patient's head to something that is also straining if not destroying a social unit.

Removal of any member of a family needs to be considered in terms of its impact on the whole group. This is not to suggest that admission is always a last resort – very far from it. But it does suggest that viewing the resident as an isolated individual is doing less than justice to the situation from which he has come, and to which he may return. The circumstances of the family itself, of course, may well be a consequence of wider social pressures, such as poor housing and unemployment. One of the difficulties faced by social workers aware of such factors is to decide at what point social work as such ends and community work or political action begins. Volumes can be and have been written on such matters (see, among many others, Halmos 1978), but for present purposes we must find a reasonable cut-off point. I suggest that it is to be found at the point at which *the particular circumstances of the client become lost in the more general considerations*. Politically oriented workers maintain that this means that social work can be no more than a palliative measure, and they may be right, but since identical problems do not beset everyone who lives in the same neighbourhood, in similarly poor accommodation, or at a similar level of poverty, it is reasonable to direct some attention to the particular needs of a particular client.

Mistakes from Boundaries Drawn too Tightly

The difficulty for the residential worker, however, is not one of knowing how to narrow the boundaries so that intervention is both practical and useful, but of widening them to include life beyond the four walls. It is easy to misjudge people when you know nothing of their background – or even, as residential workers sometimes do, when you pretend that background does not exist. Residential assessment of children and young people in care is a case in point. Behaviour tends to be seen as something that originates purely from within the young person. Much of this book has so far been about the possibility that it is in part a response to the living environment; wider than that, it may be a response to the process of being admitted to care; wider still, behaviour may be carried over from conduct developed in order to survive in a particular family, or a particular community. 'Treatment' that is designed to eradicate behaviour that seems to be deviant within the establishment may well succeed merely in de-skilling the individual so that he cannot survive 'back home'. Residential staff are beginning to respect cultural differences on a grand scale, largely because of the need for changes in routine procedure such as special diets for clients from ethnic minority groups, but there is often a neglected gap between the broad cultural dimension on the one hand and the circumstances of the particular resident on the other.

A prime example is to be found in lack of trust. This is a characteristic of a fair proportion of people who find themselves in residential provision, and is generally seen by staff as undesirable. They try to persuade residents to trust them, and they demonstrate their trustworthiness as much as they can. If the client does not respond, they are offended and regard such conduct as pathological. But if you are a child who has lived in an abusing family for far longer than you have lived in children's home or with foster parents, you do not want to trust anyone, because trust means being let down and being hurt. The same goes for the old person who has been neglected, abandoned, or even assaulted by her own family. If you do eventually trust staff or foster parents, you have to discriminate between them and the people you have known outside. Those other people suffer by the comparison, and the extra blame that is then attached to them may be even more difficult to cope with than the feeling that there is no one to trust. All this only makes sense when the lack of trust is seen within a context, as a property of a wider system than the residential establishment itself.

DRAWING THE LINE

Where the boundary is to be drawn in the practice of social work from a residential base is not easy to decide, once the 'four walls' have been abandoned. The decision depends on many factors. It clearly makes sense for the staff to work with present, potential, and former clients and their families or other natural groupings outside the establishment, while respecting their rights not to be interfered with, unless necessity and/or

clear benefit and low cost to the client can be shown for intervention in their lives. But how is that concern for the wider world
to be reconciled with the demands of what goes on inside the
establishment and, given the extra workload, the need to keep
staff groups small enough to facilitate personal relationships
between residents and staff? There are only so many hours in the
day and the working week.

Those who see residential establishments as too insular suggest
that they should be resource centres for the neighbourhood – that
staff and residents should not merely go out, but that neighbours
and community groups should come in and make use of the facilities offered. Unfortunately, this too poses a problem in the recon-
ciliation of the residents' right to privacy with the community's
right to access (Wagner 1988). Such a resource centre model
may be quite easy to reconcile with core and cluster schemes of
community care when the core is not itself a residential establishment, but is more difficult when the dependence of the residents
necessitates a fully and consistently staffed establishment.

Here again values are inescapable. Weighing the interests of
those outside in relation to (not necessarily *against*) those inside
is not merely a technical exercise, but depends on the value that
is placed on say, availability of staff for residents, the intimacy
of the residential community, and the privacy of the residents.
The values at this level are not necessarily those of the residential
staff themselves; management and local political considerations
come into play. For some patterns of provision there is no
problem; for others, the central values of the establishment
would be jeopardized by trying to turn it into something which
it is not. An establishment providing respite care is necessarily
involved with its catchment area. Good practice for such a unit
requires relationships with parents and relatives of residents at
the very least, and probably with residents' friends, with their
other contacts in the community, and perhaps with voluntary
groups. A 'home' on the other hand maintains such contacts only
on the authority of the residents, which is the same as in ordinary
families. To seal off the respite care programme is to turn it into
a sausage machine; to open up the home without the residents'
authority is to turn it into a zoo.

Transactions across Boundaries

Boundaries are not and should not be seen as impermeable. They are crossed every time someone crosses the threshold or makes a telephone call. But crossing a boundary raises issues of *management*. Some approaches to management actually regard it as primarily the regulation of transactions across boundaries:

The decision to admit someone to an establishment is a transaction across the boundary between it and the outside world, which clearly requires regulation.

Ordering food is a transaction across a boundary.

What is the difference between the two examples? Mainly, the seriousness and the implications of the transaction. Mistakes in ordering food are fairly easy to rectify, those of admitting a new resident much less so. But every time a serious decision is made, the person making it has to refer back to the task of the establishment, and it is ultimately the task that determines which boundaries are regarded as important in practice. Alternatively, by looking at which boundaries are treated as important and how they are managed, one can deduce a great deal about the task as it works in practice. Thus:

At an admissions panel for homes for elderly people, the case under consideration was an old man who was living in squalor, at least in part because of his heavy drinking. He suffered from arthritis (the pain of which may have been relieved in some measure by his drinking) and a certain amount of confusion (which may have been worsened by his drinking). His language was also colourful, to say the least. The discussion about his placement in one establishment centred around:

1. An agreement that he was a suitable candidate for care, being clearly unable to look after himself and being willing – even enthusiastic – about the idea of admission, and

2. A feeling that he was not a suitable candidate for this particular establishment on the grounds that he would not fit in with the present group of old 'ladies and gentlemen'.

There was a conflict here between accepting that the overall task of the Department was to provide for people in need – which this old man (note this distinction between 'man' and 'gentleman') clearly was – and the task of the establishment to provide a home, with congenial company, for the existing group of residents. As so often happens in these cases, the case for admission was being pushed by the Departmental managers, and the case for finding a place elsewhere by the Head of Home. Technically, it *ought* to be the case that the boundaries follow the task. In the real world what frequently happens is that some boundaries receive much more attention than others, and therefore that the task is adapted to suit the boundaries that seem to require most attention. Although from the point of view of the organization as a whole this is wrong, from the point of view of a part of the whole it may be perfectly reasonable. As in the case above, this is a frequent source of conflict between residential establishments and the agencies of which they are a part. Regardless of the rights or wrongs of the issue, it is in practice resolved on the basis of who has the authority to control the boundary around the establishment (on which basis the residents do not get a look in at all).

I have already referred to the way in which the ordering of food was handled in at least one establishment to emphasize its distinctiveness (page 44), but in many cases such ordering is the kind of routine activity that is done at a fairly low level in the management hierarchy. In many Social Services departments ordering is in any case hedged about with a number of constraints, such as pre-existing arrangements with companies that have tendered to supply certain goods, which suggest that it may be regarded as an activity that is purely technical. Even so, the management of that boundary also implies value judgements about the task.

In one authority that was making a great point of normalization as a principle of its 'care of community' programme, the group homes nevertheless had their groceries delivered weekly by a wholesaler. Everything came in catering packs, such as seven-pound cans of jam, and enormous brown boxes of corn-flakes.

Apart from the system depriving the dwellers in the group homes of the experience of doing their own shopping (and handling money, and making decisions about how much to buy, and facing the consequences of running out of things), it did not do much for the 'ordinariness' of the house to have a large truck delivering groceries every Tuesday.

Not every decision relating to a transaction across a boundary has to be taken at the highest level (on the contrary, in the last example it would be more desirable for food purchase decisions to be taken by the residents themselves), but the policy that governs such transactions does need to be sorted out by the management with the task and its associated values clearly in mind.

DEFINING THE TASK

In the preceding discussion I have referred several times to the notion of 'task', but I have not defined it. In a conventional text on the theory of organizations the definition of task would come long before a discussion of boundaries. But we are in the business of looking at what happens in practice, and while the task might be defined very broadly in the initial set-up of a project (see the story of the establishment of the old people's home, page 112ff), it almost inevitably changes as the project gets under way and as the working myth becomes more firmly established. The original aims, which provided the basic framework for the task, become displaced into the working myth, and the task itself follows them.

Rice (1958) defines the *primary task* of an enterprise as *'that task which an enterprise must perform in order to survive'*. This definition has three useful features: first, it draws attention to survival in the environment as the principal factor in determining what the enterprise must do (*e.g.* a business concern has to make a profit or at least to break even). The results of such an analysis are often rather disconcerting, because they may have very little relation to the expressed aims of the enterprise, as we shall see below.

Second, it focuses on what the enterprise *is actually doing*, not what it would like to think it is doing, which is the kind of thing set out in the aims. It therefore fits in well with our previous discussion of working myths, which have the same concern with what appears to be really going on as opposed to fantasies about what ought to be happening.

Third, however, in the case of a non-profit organization (and even some profit-making ones) it raises further important questions: (1) What constitutes survival? and (2) Who decides whether an institution is surviving or not? In the case of a residential establishment, for example, it is clearly possible for it to be closed down (which constitutes 'not surviving' in its most dramatic form), but there are other circumstances in which it might be seen to have failed to survive. Occasionally, a staff member leaves a place, saying 'It's just not the same place as the one I came to work in two (or twenty) years ago.' When do the many little changes that always accrue in the life of an establishment lead to a new kind of place superseding the old? It is the kind of change that is only recognized after the event. The name may be the same, even a large proportion of the staff and the residents may be the same, but something significant has happened (for better or for worse), which means that the whole is different.

The second question (who decides?) draws attention to the power relations within the system. It has been pointed out that ultimately even a prison can only continue to function with the consent of its inmates (Emery 1970). Everyone has their part to play in the continuing survival of the system, and on occasion this accounts for the way in which a task can become displaced from the original intention.

The Task of an Open System

In the case of a system that is clearly open to the environment, it is relatively easy to discern the primary task, because there is an end product that is different from the initial state of whatever (or whoever) went into the system. Thus in the case of a business making electrical goods, the inputs may be raw material, workers, capital, equipment, and energy; the outputs are electrical goods, employees with wages, profit or loss, and payments for the inputs. The difference between the outputs and the inputs has obviously been created by what has happened inside the intervening 'conversion system'.

There are some residential establishments that are in a sense like that. They are designed to 'export' people into the community, and it is notionally possible to evaluate them by their results.

One approach to the evaluation of establishments dealing with young offenders, such as the old approved schools or detention centres, was to look at the re-offending rates of their former residents, up to, say, three years after discharge. The trouble with this method, when applied naïvely, was that it did not take account of the changes in the nature and problems of the residents before admission and the changes in the environment. However, such analyses sometimes suggested not merely that the establishments failed to stop former residents committing offences, but that they actually trained them to do so; that their unintended achievement was to be 'schools for crime'.

Some establishments are explicitly set up as 'training units', to equip their residents to live ordinary lives, as far as they are capable, in the 'community' (i.e. outside residential care). One such establishment was a hostel for former mental patients. When asked what happened to residents after a stay at the hostel, the Head of Home disclosed that three-quarters of them returned to the hospital. It would seem therefore that what the establishment was actually doing was enabling most of its residents to learn that they *could not* survive in the community.

The hostel, however, continued to survive, as do the short, sharp shock detention centres, despite its actual record. This suggests that their *primary* task is not to do with the throughput of residents, but with something else, which is probably much more political.

There are other residential establishments that do not have

such identifiable 'outputs'. Any institution providing lifetime care, such as an old people's home, cannot even attempt to judge its performance on the basis of what happens to its residents after they leave, because most of them either go to hospital or they die. A similar situation applies in the case of an establishment catering for people with progressive disabilities. Clearly, what happens to the residents is largely (although not perhaps entirely) independent of what the establishment itself does.

In one of the most institutional old people's homes it has ever been my misfortune to come across, there had been over the years a number of residents who reached the age of 99 – but none of them ever made it to 100. It is not unreasonable to suppose that they just did not want to live to that significant milestone in that depressing atmosphere.

It is a salutary exercise for even these establishments to look at the difference between their 'inputs' and their 'outputs' over a defined period (say a month) on the basis of criteria that the clients, relatives, and staff find significant, and to see what actually happens to residents. The fact that residents do not actually leave to go on to greater things should not suggest that there are no outputs. Measuring instruments such as those developed by Moos and colleagues (1979) focus the mind wonderfully, but even simple check-lists can show up changes over time. In the light of information gathered in such a way, staff, perhaps working with an objective outsider, can then assess whether or not there is any connection between the areas into which they put most effort and devote most attention, and those that seem to be associated with effective change for the better in the experiences of residents.

Changes in the Environment

Changes in the effectiveness of residential establishments, however, are not wholly governed by factors inside them. All social systems that are at all open to the environment have to able to adapt to changes in that environment. Changes outside can make an establishment irrelevant or even counter-productive if it does not adjust to them. It makes no sense in the present day for a children's home to prepare young people for a life in domestic service, as they used to, simply because the job market no longer exists. In the 1960s many homes for elderly people were built for active and lucid residents who happened to prefer a residential environment to one in which they had to make choices for themselves. In a sense, their rather regimented regimes did not matter as much because it was easier for such residents to go out and to maintain contacts with relatives and friends. In the 1980s fewer residents are active and lucid, and the establishments have had to adapt to their changing needs as well as to changing values as to what constitutes 'good care'. Expectations change, too. People with a physical handicap are no longer content to be seen as 'cripples', and to be kept out of sight of the public. People with learning difficulties are becoming sensitive to their rights, and rejecting the label of 'mental handicap'. Residents' relatives are rightly demanding more involvement (instead of just 'putting someone away') and more complex co-operative arrangements with residential resources, often in order to enable them to keep on playing their part in caring for a handicapped member.

Establishments that operate as closed systems, ignoring the changing demands of the world outside, are vulnerable to crises in which it suddenly becomes apparent that 'we can't go on like this'. Unless they have done some analysis of what constitutes the significant tasks and boundaries of their work (however much those tasks may be intertwined with and embedded in others), such crises are likely to be experienced as global threats in which the good parts of present practice are lost as well as those that no longer fit with the changing outside world.

Each new arrival, and the circumstances of each person discharged, should make a residential establishment aware of the world from which they have come, and that to which they are going. In practice it is the ongoing work with those who are living in the 'home' that tends to assume greater importance, and instead of learning from new residents more effort goes into assimilating them into the existing system. In the terms of the earlier chapters, homoeostasis assumes greater importance than change, and order matters more than mitigation or compensatory experience.

Beyond the Primary Task

The demands of the outside world (which are significant factors establishing the level of administrative convenience) do not prevent committed staff from going beyond the primary task, but they will be engaging in a Sisyphean task if they do.

The director of an excellent centre providing three-month training programmes for young adults with a mental handicap was reputed to tell the parents of his clients: 'I can promise only one thing about your child when he completes this training programme – he will be three months older.' This was entirely realistic, if very conservative. It was said, half tongue-in-cheek, as a corrective to the fantasy that the centre could work miracles. But it certainly did not mean that the staff would not work very hard to ensure that the young man (or woman) did benefit greatly from the training opportunities offered.

Undertaking the exercise of defining the primary task of an assessment centre with a group of its staff a few years ago, the group came up with a formula that it was 'To take difficult young people off the hands of the field social workers with as little fuss as possible.' Needless to say, they found this very dispiriting, but acknowledged that no one would ever think of closing the place down as long as it continued to fulfil this function; and equally that no one in authority in their department seemed to take very much interest in the centre achieving any more than this.

THE MANAGEMENT OF BOUNDARIES

It has been suggested that the boundaries to which most attention is paid give some good clues to the *de facto* task of the system. In the case of the assessment centre cited above, this certainly applied. Despite the phrase in the analysis, 'with as little fuss as possible', the process of admission was taken much more seriously than that of discharge. Regardless of all the assessment reports that were prepared and the case conference that took place, this assessment centre was like many others in that the actual business of finding a permanent placement came down to waiting for a bed to appear in a vaguely suitable establishment, the nature of which could have been predicted with a large degree of accuracy from broad factors that were known before the young person was ever admitted to the centre. Thereafter, the transfer was effected on the basis of a couple of telephone calls and scratching around to find a field or residential worker who could drive the unfortunate young person over to the new place, accompanied by the usual carrier bags of belongings. Leaving aside the issues of good or bad practice, and concentrating purely on the organizational side, it is clear that reception assumed much more importance than discharge, and the lack of facilities for long stays in the establishment (such as adequate arrangements for education) indicated that it was also more important than the stay itself, despite the fact that stays of up to a year were not uncommon, particularly for adolescent girls.

Clues to the significance of boundaries are found in the seniority of the people who have to make the decision to cross them and the number of people who have to be consulted before such a decision can be made. Less important boundaries are marked by routinized procedures, and decisions taken at lower levels of seniority. Boundaries seen as less important than hitherto are marked by delegation, usually with the requirement that the final decision be counter-signed by a senior person.

CLIENT MOVEMENTS ACROSS BOUNDARIES

Lest it be thought that the issue of boundaries is purely a management issue for staff, we need to look at the experience of those people who are being 'processed' through the system, and at what crossing boundaries into, inside, and out of residential establishments does to them.

Admission

We have words for it: 'reception', 'admission' or even 'taking' into care. The very existence of the words, and the subtle distinctions in meaning between them, point to the extent to which the process is routine for those engaged in social work. There are legal requirements, codes of practice, procedure files, forms to fill in, and standard letters, which not only help to ensure a consistent standard of practice, but also act for those involved as defences against the recognition of the seriousness or even enormity of the step being taken (Brearley *et al.* 1980).

The client has no such defences, and probably no previous experience of what to expect. Admissions very often take place at moments of crisis when the client's personal resources are at a low ebb, if she or he can understand what is happening at all. Consider the following scenario, if you want to imagine what it is like to go into care. (I have chosen this particular one because it is plausible for adult professionals and does not refer to an establishment you are as likely to be familiar with as some other scenarios. I hope that it never happens to you.)

For some reason your world has fallen apart, and you have fallen into the depths of depression, possibly because of a loss of some kind. Life is terrible and dark. You can occasionally summon up the energy to 'cheer up' when some determined person needs you to do so, to make them feel better, but inside you feel chaotic and lost and hopeless and there is no light at the end of the tunnel. The darkness is getting deeper and is full of some nameless dread which threatens you. You cannot sleep, you cannot work, you are irritated by everything and everyone around you, and you have no energy for anything. It has crossed your mind to kill yourself but you have not even got the energy for that.

Someone suggests going to the doctor. He smiles and gives you pills but they do not help. Later they suggest hospital. You know that means a mental hospital. People out here are bad enough, but what would it be like to be surrounded by mad people all the time? And people who go in there never come out, do they? Even if they do, no one ever accepts that they are 'normal' again, do they? You will not go, and make a defiant effort to get better so that it will not happen. You cannot sustain it, and collapse in weeping exhaustion. The doctor visits and tries to persuade you; you hardly have the strength to answer. A psychiatrist comes round, examines you briefly, and says you really ought to go in – you can either come of your own accord or it may be necessary to force you. It gets worse. You are losing control over everything. No one listens any more. The family has rows about you. Now a social worker comes and insists on talking to you and then goes away to whisper to the rest of the family. They are going to put you away regardless! You will be abandoned. No one cares. An ambulance comes; the ambulance men are kind but firm. They listen to the social worker, not to you. What will happen? What will become of me?

The story is a common one. The prospective patient was probably given a lot of information and reassurance but could not take it in. *It is not surprising if the state of that person on arrival at hospital or residential establishment is worse than it was before* (Blenkner 1967). Good practice calls for taking whatever steps are appropriate to mitigate the trauma of admission, such as pre-admission visits to the establishment, special arrangements for welcome, and efforts to maintain a degree of continuity with the new resident's previous life, but these can do little to overcome the powerful feelings of loss and anxiety that are likely to accompany crossing the boundary into the new home (see Marris (1986) for a fuller discussion of loss and change).

Even when admission is a matter of choice and perhaps welcomed by the new resident, it is still a crisis and issues of management are raised. Crisis theory (Caplan 1964; Murgatroyd and Woolfe 1982) suggests that people in crisis are disoriented, vulnerable, and open to change in a way that people in non-crisis situations are not. Crisis may in part be defined as a state in which established coping mechanisms prove inadequate to the situation. This opens a number of issues and possibilities for the residential practitioner:

1. Assessment of a new resident immediately on admission is

not likely to tell you very much about their normal state, even at a physical level – blood pressure may be up and heart-rate increased as a result of anxiety, for example. Psychologically, a confused person is almost certain to appear more confused; a person with a mental handicap may temporarily (or permanently) lose some capacities and skills that have been painfully acquired; a young person may regress or assume a brittle bravado. Depression is a *normal*, rather than a pathological response. So is attention-seeking. As one very wise and experienced practitioner put it, 'I fail to understand why some young people in care are *not* attention-seekers!' Anger is understandable, to say the least. The absence of such reactions may be more of a cause for concern than their presence. The experience of being admitted for reasons beyond one's control and with no control of the process creates helplessness and depression (Seligman 1974).

2. Superficial coping is established much sooner than real psychological coping. Staff tend to assume that as soon as the new resident has learned his way around the building, familiarized himself with routines and basic rules, and learned the names of one or two people, the admission crisis is over – he has 'settled in'. Not so. Many people may never feel 'at home' in their new situation, and although time may be distorted so that after a few days a resident will tell staff, 'I feel as if I've been here for years', the process of mourning takes much longer than that to accomplish. It may be weeks or months before a resident is his 'old self' again, if indeed he is ever allowed to rediscover that old self, and has not been 'taken over' by the culture of the establishment.

3. Some organizations consciously exploit the suggestibility of the disorientated new recruit to impress their own stamp on him. Initiation rituals may be designed to humiliate him, and leave him in no doubt as to the power of the organization and his own insignificance (LaFontaine 1985), or they may increase his commitment to the culture. Having to struggle to gain entry is one way in which it is made more likely that a person will be committed to a group he has joined, and initiation may be carried out within the resident subculture as well as within the

formal structure of the establishment (Wills 1971; Yablonsky 1967). This may be seen as a way of providing a Shell for someone who has over-extended himself into his Skeleton. It presents two problems for the staff: first, the management of the subcultural influences if they are at variance with those of the establishment itself, and second, the danger of being so 'caring' about what the resident is going through that his dependence is reinforced and he comes to believe that being dependent is 'the way to behave' in the establishment.

Leaving

If admission to residential provision is a recognized crisis and trauma, leaving it is just as much of one, and in many respects it is exactly the same kind of crisis. It involves transition across a boundary that affects every aspect of the former resident's life. It is characterized by the same kind of ambivalence of fear and excited anticipation, but because it is generally seen by social work staff as a move to something 'better' (it is the conventional wisdom that living on the basis of one's own Skeleton is better than dependence on someone else's Shell), such fears are often not acknowledged explicitly, but expressed instead in covert ways. There may be increasing acceptance by professionals of the need to prepare people for 'independent' living, but this is seen largely as a matter of knowledge and skills, and the feelings tend to be neglected. (For a fuller discussion of the issues see Brearley *et al.* 1982.) On the basis that the attention paid to boundary management and the actual task of the establishment are closely linked, it is not surprising to find that the closed-system thinking identified earlier means that only in specialized units does the matter of leaving (which is different from 'discharge', which is the institutional perspective on the process) receive the attention it deserves from the point of view of the resident.

We may expect, therefore, that as the time to leave approaches, the resident, who is being expected to learn or re-learn a variety of skills, will at the same time find it difficult to learn them because his feelings get in the way. Even if he is not imaginative enough to be worried about the prospect of leaving, there is the likelihood that under the stress of having to rely on his Skeleton he may well forget much that he has learned. There is a tension for the residential staff, too, in the preparation process. How seriously are they permitted to take the risk-taking element of this learning?

It is not uncommon in independence-training units for young people about to leave care for a calculation of their rent to be made on the basis of their income. They are allowed a certain amount for food and possibly for heating, for travelling to work (if they are in work), for pocket-money, and so on. The rent is then calculated on the basis of what is left over.

In the 'real world', of course, the situation is reversed: the landlord has first claim on the tenant's income (even if supplemented by Housing Benefit), and the tenant then has to make do with what is left. If he has no pocket-money to buy his records or his cigarettes, then that is unfortunate. Eviction for non-payment of rent may be a lengthy and complicated process, particularly in the case of council tenants who would otherwise be made homeless, but it is nonetheless a possibility. While the client is technically in care, however, eviction is not a live option. The agency is still accountable for what happens to their client and can therefore not expose him to the consequences of his actions which would apply in the 'real world'. (See also pages 77–8.)

The effect of this continuing Shell protection is that the actual move out of care still comes as a crisis. Since crises are occasions of learning, it is a moot point whether they should be anticipated in such a way as to minimize their effects, but it is nonetheless important to contain them so that they do not create problems that the individual cannot cope with. The difficulty for the worker is that containment is by definition a Shell activity, and the more that crises are contained by someone other than the individual himself, the more difficult it becomes to move into Skeleton. This situation is often exploited in the phenomenon known in the prison service as 'gate fever' and in

Transactional Analysis as the game of 'How do you get out of here?' (Berne 1966).

A young man in a Community Home with Education was getting ready to leave to go into lodgings at the age of about 17½. Although he had a record of theft and other offences, and had been in the school for about three years, his behaviour for the past year or so had been exemplary. He was overtly enthusiastic about his departure; he talked excitedly to other residents and staff about his bed-sitter (which he had been to see), and his plans for his life when he had got out of 'this dump'. Two weeks before his leaving date, he went into the local town and stole an expensive leather coat from a store which had an alarm-tag system. He was of course picked up by the store detective at the exit, and handed over to the police.

Not only did this young man put his chances of discharge at risk, he also did so in a conspicuously stupid manner. Although he said that he did not know about the alarm system, it was very obvious that he did. He was effectively trying to force the authorities to continue to hold him (in two senses). He may not have been conscious of the side of himself that was worried about leaving care, but it came out anyway. Apart from the legal considerations of how the theft ought to be dealt with, the Department was faced with the double bind of whether to hold him responsible for the theft and thereby probably to end up keeping him in care, which would preserve him from other kinds of responsibility, or to continue with their plans for his discharge at the potential cost of telling him that he was in some sense not *really* responsible for the theft.

The aftermath of leaving can be similarly fraught. Just as there may be a regressive dip in a person's capabilities on admission to care, the same problems may emerge in the transition to independence. There is the continuing danger of the agency being caught up in a first-order change process if they help out too much, and the danger on the other side of secondary problems setting in if inadequate support is given. None of these observations should be taken as statements of the inherent incapacity of former residents to cope in the outside world, but as features of what happens when such momentous transitions are made across boundaries. A similar phenomenon has been known to occur in the case of staff.

Several years ago, when it was more common for staff to be resident in their establishments than is the case now, the Head of an old people's home left to become a tutor. She had been living in a flat attached to the establishment, and paying emoluments that entitled her to draw on the home's stocks for her food. She commented later how when she moved she was suddenly panic-stricken by the thought that she would now have to make sure that she shopped for herself. She bought a catering-size freezer, and used the home's cash-and-carry card to stock it full before she actually moved out.

CONCLUSION

It is the all-embracing nature of the residential enterprise – even that which is based on 'ordinary housing', minimal staffing, and the principles of normalization – that makes the boundaries with the environment so significant. Whatever the nature of the residential provision, there are always discontinuities between the values 'inside' and those 'outside', if only in the sense that the establishment is geared to meeting the needs of the residents, whereas they do not assume such priority in the rest of the world. A children's home, for example, is supposed to revolve around the children, whereas in a family the adults take pride of place at least as often as the children do.

Normalization suggests that these differences should be minimized but there are occasions on which the different value base is precisely what makes the residential experience so valuable. The therapeutic community that emphasizes immediate confrontation over things that are 'let pass' in the rest of the world; the asylum (in the true sense) or the retreat that gives people a breathing space from routine pressures; the establishment for people with a mental handicap that can gear its pace and its patience to their learning capacities – all are necessarily different from their environment, and the difficulties they encounter where they 'interface' with that environment are necessary features. Those difficulties are far from sufficient to invalidate what they achieve, as long as the transitions across the boundaries are managed with sufficient sensitivity to ensure that the gains from residence are not lost by the process of entering or leaving.

10 Application and Change

It may be that by this stage in the book, the reader's overall reaction is that it is all very interesting, but so what? Since the object of the exercise was to provide some tools that could be used in the assessment and development of residential establishments, I ought to say something at this stage about how to use them.

Any set of tools can be used alongside others. In this book I have concentrated on the residential establishment as a *whole*, and I have been very general. Any comprehensive approach to studying residential settings, however, must make use of other perspectives as well. There is a great deal of material that is more specific to particular kinds of establishment (see the excellent collection of papers in Sinclair 1988). There is the perspective of psychology, developmental, general and social, which can direct attention to personal and interpersonal processes. The environment cannot be understood without sociological insights and the disciplines of social administration. Management processes require knowledge of organization theory, and so on. And from a personal standpoint, I believe that all residential workers should know something of philosophy.

The tools in this book are useful primarily for assessing the health of a residential establishment as a whole. They do not yield check-lists that will enable a staff member, a consultant, an inspector, or a resident automatically to give a place a score or a grading, but they do suggest terms in which the well-being of the establishment can be discussed. They may suggest areas to look at to locate the problems, which are not always where they first appear to be, and they may give some kind of guidance as to how to go about effecting change.

HOW TO USE THE TOOLS

Each of the tools is intended to be capable of standing alone, and to be used as such. The decision as to how to apply them will depend in large measure on how they resonate with you as a practitioner in your particular situation.

Which tool to use first will depend on what you want to do. In many cases, I hope that the book will have confirmed you in what you are already doing, but perhaps raised some questions about a few aspects of practice. Although it is difficult to change single aspects of the life of a residential establishment without inducing consequential change in other parts, particularly in issues at the level of generality raised by this book, that should not inhibit you from trying, as long as you are aware that you may be starting on a long haul.

At a boys' Community Home with Education, it was the practice for the boys to clean their house units before crossing to the main dining-hall for breakfast. This always meant that the cleaning was rushed, and it was felt that they should have their breakfast first and then clean the houses before going to school. This in turn meant that the catering staff would have to come in earlier; this was not acceptable and so it was decided that the boys would eat breakfast in the units. This in turn contributed to the boys identifying with the house units more at the expense of the school as a whole, and it became desirable to reorganize the staffing allocation so that individual staff links with the house units were strengthened. This meant that the staff got to know individual boys better, and shifted the disciplinary emphasis of the school from impersonal rules to a pattern based more on personal relationships with the staff. When the 'key worker' system was introduced later, it took off easily because it had a suitable infrastructure.

Skeletons and Shells

For many purposes the Skeleton and Shell model is the simplest tool to use, of those outlined here. It is relatively easy to communicate to colleagues and to apply to the life of an establishment, it seeks to account for some of the external pressures as well as the psychological issues within the establishment, and it encourages a degree of flexibility on the part of the staff. By examining the daily routine in terms of Skeleton and Shell factors, it is possible to identify areas in which change may be instituted without necessarily having to embark on a wholesale disruption. You can even undertake a Skeleton-Shell 'audit' relatively simply by getting colleagues to 'score' different features of the daily routine, or aspects of residents' behaviour, along the continuum.

If you wish to teach the Skeleton and Shell model to staff members in order to use it more effectively, you might find some of the following exercises useful.

The first one is simply designed to get a group talking about their Skeleton and Shell assumptions. Give brief sketches of a number of potential candidates for some kind of social Shell. Ask participants to decide on the strength of the Shell the people need, only on the basis of the information supplied. Use a simple 1-to-5 rating scale to assess how much of a Shell is needed, compare the 'scores', and discuss the conclusions and the reasons for them.

The next exercise moves the focus onto your own establishment. In small groups, consider your establishment in terms of the extent to which it provides a social Shell:

1. On a scale between 1 and 10 (1 for practically no Shell elements, 10 for a complete Shell), where would you put the establishment?
2. What are the factors that push it in the direction of Shell working?
3. What are the elements of Skeleton functioning that persist?

You could adapt the kind of questions about residents and procedures suggested in my book on supervision (Atherton 1986) to focus on Skeleton and Shell issues for particular people and policies.

Alternatively, you could use the analysis of residents' transition across boundaries in the previous chapter to help review admission and discharge procedures and see how these specific aspects might be prepared for, managed, and followed up.

COMPREHENSIVE REVIEW

If you wish to undertake a comprehensive review of the working of an establishment, the first thing is probably to work out what the primary task is (Chapter 9).

1. Under what circumstances might this establishment be closed down (in its presently recognizable form)?
2. What does this tell you about the functions it is *obliged* to perform?
3. What transactions across the boundary *have* to be managed by senior staff, in the eyes of:
   (a) people within the establishment, and
   (b) the powers-that-be outside it?
4. What boundary transactions consume most time and energy? How do the answers to 3 and 4 relate to that to 2?

This analysis should set out the parameters within which the establishment has to work, and which contribute to the level of administrative convenience in your particular establishment. To determine that level fully, however, demands a consideration of internal factors as well as external demands.

Think back on the changes that have been made or attempted in the recent past, and consider what happened to them.

Were they greeted with enthusiasm and readily adopted?

Or were they resisted, either successfully or unsuccessfully (an unsuccessfully resisted change may well be incorporated into the level of administrative convenience, unless it has carried with it a degree of covert resentment)?

Consider the values that were implicit in the changes, and

the demands that were made on the staff by introducing them.

Those considerations will help to map out the nature of the 'snowball' and 'Sisyphus' slopes on either side of the valley of administrative convenience. Consider too the behaviour of the senior staff or the instigators of the changes: What were they prepared to put themselves out for? Why? What made it so important?

Although the discussion has concentrated on administrative convenience as the 'lowest common denominator' of practice, it can exist at a number of levels. In an establishment where there are few external demands (or a subcultural resistance to unrealistic external demands), and little internal pressure for the improvement of practice, the level of administrative convenience will be fairly low. In one where there are either strong external requirements for high-quality provision, or perhaps the stimulus of being in the marketplace, and an internal concern with quality of service, the level will be much higher. It is technically merely the point at which least effort needs to be expended to keep the establishment running smoothly.

The Level of Functioning

The next stage, therefore, is to discover something of the level of administrative convenience in more absolute rather than relative terms. This can be done in a variety of ways, including measuring performance against standard indicators, such as criteria of normalization, or the kind of check-list of features of an old people's home found in the National Consumer Study of 100 Old People's Homes (Willcocks, Peace, and Kellaher 1987), or more broadly against principles such as the 'five C's' of the Wagner report (1988). Alternatively, the 'staircase' model (Chapter 4) may be used. It can either be the basis for reflection or discussion, or it may be interpreted more rigorously (if more simplistically) by a time-sampling exercise in which the activity of staff over set periods of time is allocated to one of the four different levels. Such an exercise would need to be interpreted sensitively, of course, in the light of the physical or order demands made by the particular resident group; but it is important that excuses should not be made for low-level practice simply on that basis.

One of the practical difficulties is determining to which step a certain bit of work by staff should be allocated, particularly whether it belongs to the order step or to a higher one. Some guidance on this may be found by adopting the homoeostasis or thermostat model (Chapter 3), and working with staff on what they take to be an acceptable level of 'social temperature' within the establishment, as well as looking at the nature of their communication with residents and with each other, in the terms of Chapter 2.

One method of doing this is to set up a series of mini-case-studies (or trigger-incidents) describing situations that might happen within your establishment (naming the people concerned if necessary), and asking staff what they would do about them, and why. If you can put aside your own assumptions, which might make the answers seem obvious, you may be able to discover the underlying norms and 'social temperature' being aimed at.

The net result of all this is likely to be simply a picture of what is in practice believed to be important in the life of the establishment. All being well (which it rarely is), such questioning should expose the working myth behind the bland statements that people in residential work often make about what they are doing. This is not to impute dishonesty to staff, but simply to suggest that very often they do not actually *know* what they are doing. Evidence to suggest that this is common has been found in the development of computer-based 'expert systems'. If even world-renowned practitioners are asked about how they go about designing an electronic circuit or diagnosing abdominal pain, the answers they give are quite likely to be very different from what they are observed to do in practice by an analyst trying to capture their decision-making expertise in a computer program. What develops from this exercise is frequently unsettling, particularly if staff have been relatively content and reflective in their work, (Willcocks, Peace, and

Kellaher (1987:128) came up with the interesting finding that in some old people's homes, the more satisfied the residents were, the less so the staff.)

USING AN OUTSIDER

Outsiders are invaluable in the process of analysis. Their main advantage is that they do not have a vested interest in the status quo. They can ask naïve questions, which frequently expose taken-for-granted aspects of practice that insiders might never have thought to mention, and they generally require insiders to explain themselves, which sometimes leads them to say things that surprise even themselves.

There are certain principles to bear in mind when bringing in an outsider. The first is that the terms of reference should be clear. Apart from the virtues of having a proper contract (and much of the reasoning behind supervision contracts applies in this context too; Atherton 1986), the act of working out the terms of reference both internally with a staff team and externally with the outsider can refine problems considerably. The second is that the outsider should not be a member of the direct line management team for the establishment; there are many things that such managers can do, but offering this kind of consultancy tends not to be one of them, simply because staff and even residents may be inhibited. The third requirement is that the outsider should be broadly in sympathy with the values that you *think* you hold, but equally should not be so wedded to a particular method of working as to be inclined to sell it to you whether appropriate or not. People who espouse a particular philosophy of care have a great deal to offer once you have decided on the direction in which you wish to go, but not until then. Brown (1984) provides a very useful guide to the use of consultancy.

CONSCIOUSNESS-RAISING AND CHANGE

If the analysis is carried out in a committed spirit by a staff team, then the exercise itself may be the stimulus for change. The team may well discover things about their practice that they are not very happy with, and be inclined to initiate change. But consciousness-raising may not be enough. It may be that not all the team will accept the findings; it may be that some or all members fall back on blaming others as a defence. There is a great deal to be said for setting up the ground rule that blaming is not permitted, but even so problems can be projected and splits in the team may be exposed (see Chapter 2).

It has to be recognized that the present system, whatever it is and however unsatisfactory and grumbled about, has a great deal of inertia, and that change cannot be achieved without cost. Ultimately, directly or indirectly, the working myth has to change if permanent change is to be effected. It may be that the appropriate strategy is to address this directly, and to look for a different paradigm on which relations with residents can be based, but exhortation is unlikely to be enough. It may be that considered structural changes need to be introduced, assiduously promoted and not allowed to drop, and carefully monitored. From a systems point of view, the ideal change will be one that will destabilize the current system and force a change in the working myth. The planning of such changes within groups is the underlying principle of systemic family therapy (Palazzoli *et al*. 1978; Fisch *et al*. 1982). Finding the right change to promote is not an easy task, however. The system may compensate for change in one direction in one part with unforeseen change in another direction in another part. The destabilization may result in a period of chaos that is unacceptable because it upsets the continuity of care for the residents, or cannot be contained by the agency management, or the whole thing may provoke a reaction that merely reinforces the staff (and resident) consensus that the old way of working was the only possible way. Remember that residents can carry the culture of an establishment more effectively than the staff, and that changing to work on a new basis is likely to upset them, which raises the ethical question of the extent to which you are entitled to disturb their lives simply in order to promote your vision of something better.

I do not want the previous paragraph to be read as a counsel of despair. Residential establishments *can* be changed, for better or for worse. In the better-known cases (Wills 1971; Jones 1982; Burton 1988; among others) the major factor has been the vision of the head of the establishment, and commentators tend to take refuge in the 'charismatic' qualities of such a leader. Such a vision is without doubt a very necessary ingredient, as Chapter 5 suggests, but personal charisma is not really an adequate explanation. In the final analysis it may not even be a desirable form of leadership, because it tends to die with the person of the leader, as Max Weber noted long ago (1970).

PROMOTING CHANGE

In practical terms, the promotion of change involves moving on a number of fronts at once, after a certain amount of preliminary work.

Preparing the ground

The first step in the preliminary work (which may also be a part of the change process itself) is that you, and the others working with you for the change, should ensure that you have the energy and the capacity to take it on. There are two ways in which this might be achieved: first by becoming superhuman (which is unlikely), and second by 'tuning' your own job so that you have the spare time to devote to the project. It is important that this is not done by exporting work to other people, because when the change gets under way, they too are going to require some extra energy. Delegation may be a useful device, but it needs to be carried out by making decisions at the lowest practicable level in the hierarchy, rather than getting other people to do your job for you. They can only make such decisions if they are clear about the policies of the establishment.

I was recently speaking to the head of a large residential establishment who had moved on. I asked him whom the agency was likely to appoint to replace him. 'I hope, no one,' he replied. 'If I've done my job properly they will not need anyone. I have been working for the past ten years to make my job redundant.'

Such reasoning may be over-sanguine, but it illustrates the principle. He had so organised the day-to-day running of the establishment that he was free to devote himself to longer-term developments. A senior member of staff can only make such a change if she can get away from needing to feel indispensable and if she can envisage such future change.

The second element in the preliminary work is to find a source of personal support and supervision.

The third element is to identify the opinion-formers within the staff group. It is likely that such people will most clearly embody the working myth as it is currently practised, and that as they change their view of it others will follow. Opinion-formers are not necessarily those in positions of formal leadership, but people who set the tone of discussions in the staff group, particularly in informal situations. If circumstances do not allow you to work with the staff group as a whole, it is the opinion-formers who must be involved with you as you plan the changes.

Starting Changes

Now undertake the analysis, using the tools discussed, and in consultation with others. Your findings should also help you to clarify areas in which the establishment is falling short of your vision and aims. Now draw up a list of things that have to be changed in terms of procedures as well as attitudes and face-to-face practices. The list should be at a low level of abstraction. Not: Residents should have more privacy, but:

Staff should knock on doors and wait for an answer before entering residents' rooms, and
Cleaning rotas should be arranged so as not to turf residents out of their rooms unnecessarily, and
Staff should not go into residents' cupboards and wardrobes

unless absolutely necessary and then only with residents' permission.

and so on.

Tick off this list those items that can be changed immediately without having too many implications for other areas of practice, and institute those changes first, paying attention to any backsliding attributable to anything other than sheer forgetfulness on the part of staff. If not everything can be done at once, balance the potential benefits to residents against the effort required to make the changes. Obviously the greater the benefit for the less effort, the higher the priority for the change.

More Radical Change

So far, there is nothing at all original in the change process. It is only when these relatively trivial changes (in the organizational terms) have been made, so that some aspects of the structure have been made ready to receive the more radical changes, that you can move on to the next stages.

Throughout the book, one underlying assumption has been that things stay as they are because the people involved get some kind of pay-off for keeping them that way. Often values and practice are compromises between conflicting demands, but even so the present practices must be yielding sufficient satisfaction for them not to have been changed already. It may be that residents and staff would get more and better pay-offs from acting differently, but the 'better the devil you know' philosophy inhibits them from experimenting. Frequently the pay-offs in the present situation are difficult to detect because they are hard to understand. It takes someone with the insight of Isobel Menzies to detect how a social system may function as a defence against anxiety (1967), or of Eric Berne (1966) to suggest that the pay-offs may not be 'good' feelings, but merely familiar ones. The working myth may give some guidance as to what the pay-offs are, but it must be said that they do not leap out at you.

(The use of the term 'pay-off' suggests that activity is

instrumental (directed towards some end) rather than *expressive* or undertaken for its own sake. In group terms, however, it is usually possible to uncover an instrumental component even in expressive activity.)

If the analysis and consciousness-raising approach works on its own, when the staff team as a whole come to a consensus that things must change because they have understood their present activity in a new light, it is because they have glimpsed new or more pay-offs in a different way of working.

The reason for identifying the pay-offs (which is not an essential step, but a useful one) is that any new pattern of working will have either to provide the same pay-offs, or to provide better ones and to supplant the present ones. The latter scenario is the more likely and the more difficult, and is basically the group counterpart of the process of 'threatening learning' described in an earlier book (Atherton 1986). Angyal (1965) suggests that the process through which one system takes over from another is that the 'new' system gradually saps the energy of the 'old' one, and the new grows at the expense of the old until it takes over completely.

There are three fronts on which you can move to achieve this supplantation, although it will not be easy. The first is by the use of staff support systems, such as staff meetings and individual and group supervision, to 'undermine' the need for defensive practice. The second is by re-casting the *language* of the staff team by consistently talking in terms of the new value system or working myth, and encouraging others to do so. The terminology of this book and its models may contribute to this process. The third is through the structural changes that progressively reflect the new value system rather than the old one, and the consequential changes in working practices that 'lock' the new ways of doing things into place and make them more difficult to undo.

The fact that the overall process can be described in one brief paragraph does not mean that it is quick or simple. It is a Sisyphean task, and may take months or years to accomplish completely, particularly when you encounter testing-out, backlashes, and the sort of *reductio ad absurdum* caricature of the values and practice you are trying to encourage, which seems to make a mockery of everything you stand for. (If you do not recognize this particular backlash pattern, try making the changes, and you probably soon will!)

In this discussion, I have deliberately not used examples, for fear that they would suggest that there is a recipe to be followed, and that the pattern is the same in all settings. That is clearly not the case, but by casting the suggested strategy at a fairly high level of abstraction I hope that it can be applied in many different settings. For further accounts of change processes in residential settings, see Kennard (1986).

CONCLUSION

Change requires commitment and preparedness to pay the price, and having tools to undertake a preliminary analysis is only the first step on a long road. But changes are afoot in the current environment of residential work, too. They may well force change both directly and indirectly. The emphasis in the Wagner report on consumer choice and the preservation of rights, as well as new directions in community care programmes, means that staying still and maintaining a comfortably smooth-running establishment is no longer as viable an option as it was. Nevertheless, I must conclude by returning to my original theme: that all this technical paraphernalia is just a necessary device to help people to translate values into practice. Technical change, no matter how sophisticated, is valueless without such underpinnings. We may all have different ideas about what makes for a good life, for residents as well as for ourselves. Despite our best efforts, there is no way in which we can avoid imposing our values on those with whom we work – even an emphasis on choice and rights is a staff value position. The least we can do is to be clear about those values, and to ensure that what we believe in is not diluted or even contradicted by a service delivery system that takes on a life of its own and subjugates us all to it. The final question and tool for analysis is, to what extent does residential provision suffer from the Frankenstein effect?

Bibliography

Adorno, T., Frenkel-Brunswick, E., Levinson, D.J., and Sanford, R.N. (1983) *The Authoritarian Personality*, New York: Norton.

Angyal, A. (1985) *Neurosis and Treatment*, New York: Wiley.

Argyris, C. and Schön, D.A. (1974) *Theory in Practice: increasing professional effectiveness*, San Francisco, CA: Jossey-Bass.

Atherton, J.S. (1982) 'Wave the wand', *Social Work Today* 14, no. 9:19.

——— (1983) 'No smoke without fire', *Social Work Today* 14, no. 40:19.

——— (1984) 'Never give up on a good thing', *Social Work Today* 15, no. 32:19.

——— (1986) *Professional Supervision in Group Care*, London: Tavistock.

Baron, C. (1984) 'The Paddington Day Hospital: crisis and control in a therapeutic institution', *International Journal of Therapeutic Communities* 5, no. 3:157–70.

——— (1985) 'A reply to Richard Crockett', *International Journal of Therapeutic Communities* 6, no. 2:115–18.

Bateson, G. (1973) *Steps to an Ecology of Mind*, London: Paladin.

Beedell, C. (1970) *Residential Life with Children*, London: Routledge & Kegan Paul.

Benedict, R. (1967) *The Chrysanthemum and the Sword*, London: Routledge & Kegan Paul.

Berger, P.L. (1961) *The Precarious Vision*, New York: Doubleday.

Berne, E. (1966) *Games People Play*, London: Andre Deutsch.

Berridge, D. (1985) *Children's Homes*, Oxford: Basil Blackwell.

Berry, J. (1975) *Daily Experience in Residential Life: a study of children and their care-givers*, London: Routledge & Kegan Paul.

Bettenson, C. (1943) *Documents of the Christian Church*, Oxford: OUP.

Bion, W.R. (1970) *Attention and Interpretation*, London: Tavistock.

Blenkner, M. (1967) 'Environmental change and the ageing individual', *The Gerontologist* 7, no. 3:101–5.

Bramham, P. (1980) *How Staff Rule*, Farnborough: Saxon House.

Brearley, P., Hall, F., Guttridge, P., Jones, G., and Roberts, F. (1980) *Admission into Residential Care*, London: Tavistock.

Brearley, P., Black, S., Guttridge, P., Roberts, G., and Tarrun, E. (1982) *Leaving Residential Care*, London: Tavistock.

Brickman, P., Rabinowitz, V.C., Karuza, J., Coates, D., Cohn, E., and Kidder, L. (1982) 'Models of helping and coping', *American Psychologist* 37, no. 4:368–84.

Brown, A. (1984) *Consultation: an aid to successful social work*, London: Heinemann/Community Care.

212 *Interpreting Residential Life*

Buckholdt, D.R. and Gubrium, J.F. (1979) *Caretakers: treating emotionally disturbed children*, Beverly Hills, CA: Sage.

Burton, J. (1988) 'Change from the inside', *Social Work Today*, 28 January, 11 February, 25 February 1988.

Cameron, J. (1988) 'Sense and security – should staff lock themselves away?' *Social Work Today*, 7 January 1988.

Camus, A. (1975) *The Myth of Sisyphus*, Harmondsworth: Penguin.

Caplan, G. (1964) *Principles of Preventive Psychiatry*, London: Tavistock.

Carter, R., Martin, J., Mayblin, B., and Munday, M. (1984) *Systems, Management and Change*, London: Harper & Row/Open University.

Cherry, C. (1980) *On Human Communication*, Cambridge, MA: MIT Press.

Clough, R. (1981) *Old Age Homes*, London: Allen & Unwin.

Crockett, R. (1985) 'On Claire Baron's paper, "The Paddington Day Hospital: crisis and control in a therapeutic institution"', *International Journal of Therapeutic Communities* 6, no. 2:109–14.

Crowther, M.A. (1983) *The Workhouse System, 1834–1929: the history of an English social institution*, London: Methuen.

Cumming, E. and Henry, W.E. (1961) *Growing Old: the process of disengagement*, New York: Basic Books.

Curran, C.A. (1972) *Counselling-Learning: a whole-person model for education*, New York: Grune & Stratton.

Dally, P. and Connolly, J. (1981) *Physical Methods of Treatment in Psychiatry* (6th edn), London: Churchill Livingstone.

Davis, A. (1981) *The Residential Solution*, London: Tavistock.

Douglas, M. (1973) *Natural Symbols*, Harmondsworth: Penguin.

Douglas, T. (1986) *Group Living*, London: Tavistock.

Emery, F.E. (1970) *Freedom and Justice within Walls: the Bristol prison experiment*, London: Tavistock.

Erickson, E. (1965) *Childhood and Society*, Harmondsworth: Penguin.

Fisch, R., Weakland, J.H., and Segal, L. (1982) *The Tactics of Change: doing therapy briefly*, New York: Norton.

Fordham, F. (1966) *An Introduction to Jung's Psychology*, Harmondsworth: Penguin.

Furnham, A. and Bochner, S. (1986) *Culture Shock: psychological reactions to unfamiliar environments*, London: Methuen.

Goffman, E. (1968) *Asylums: essays on the social situation of mental patients and other inmates*, Harmondsworth: Penguin.

—— (1971) *The Presentation of Self in Everyday Life*, Harmondsworth, Penguin.

—— (1975) *Frame Analysis*, Harmondsworth: Penguin.

Halmos, P. (1978) *The Personal and the Political*, London: Constable.

Hargreaves, D. (1972) *Interpersonal Relations and Education*, London: Routledge & Kegan Paul.

Havighurst, R.J. and Albrecht, R. (1953) *Older People*, New York: Longman.

Hinshelwood, R. (1982) 'The mystic and the group', *International Journal of*

Therapeutic Communities 3, no. 3:121–5.

Hobbes, T. (1981) *Leviathan*, Harmondsworth: Penguin.

Holden, U.P. and Woods, R.T. (1982) *Reality Orientation: psychological approaches to the 'confused' elderly*, Edinburgh: Churchill Livingstone.

Jones, K. and Fowles, A.J. (1984) *Ideas on Institutions: analysing the literature of long-term care and custody*, London: Routledge & Kegan Paul.

Jones, M. (1978) *The Maturation of the Therapeutic Community*, New York: Human Sciences Press.

—— (1982) *The Process of Change*, London: Routledge & Kegan Paul.

Kelly, G. (1955) *The Psychology of Personal Constructs*, New York: W.W. Norton.

Kennard, D. (1983) *An Introduction to Therapeutic Communities*, London: Routledge & Kegan Paul.

—— (1986) 'Models of institutional change – a preliminary sketch' *International Journal of Therapeutic Communities* 7, no. 3:165–75.

Klein, M. (1958) *Our Adult World and Other Essays*, London: Heinemann Medical.

Koestler, A. (1976) *The Ghost in the Machine*, London: Hutchinson.

Kuhn, T.S. (1970) *The Structure of Scientific Revolutions*, Chicago, IL: University of Chicago Press.

LaFontaine, J. (1985) *Initiation*, Harmondsworth: Penguin.

Laing, R.D. (1972) *Knots*, Harmondsworth: Penguin.

Main, T. (1975) 'Some psychodynamics of large groups', in L. Kreeger (ed.), *The Large Group: dynamics and therapy*, London: Constable.

Mannheim, K. (1954) *Ideology and Utopia*, London: Routledge & Kegan Paul.

Marris, P. (1986) *Loss and Change* (rev. edn), London: Routledge & Kegan Paul.

Maslow, A. (1987) *Motivation and Personality* (3rd edn), New York: Harper & Row.

Menzies, I.E.P. (1967) *A Case-study in the Functioning of Social Systems as a Defence against Anxiety*, London: Tavistock, pamphlet no. 3.

Miller, E.J. and Gwynne, G.V. (1972) *A Life Apart*, London: Tavistock.

Moos, R.H., Gauvain, M., Lemke, S., Max, W., and Mehren, B. (1979) 'Assessing the social environments of sheltered care settings', *The Gerontologist* 19, no. 1:74–82.

Murgatroyd, S. and Woolfe, M. (1982) *Coping with Crisis*, London: Harper & Row.

Musgrove, F. (1964) *Youth and the Social Order*, London: Routledge & Kegan Paul.

Oswin, M. (1971) *The Empty Hours*, Harmondsworth: Penguin.

Palazzoli, M.S., Boscolo, L., Cecchin, G., and Prata, G. (1978) *Paradox and Counter-Paradox*, New York: Aronson.

Parker, R.A. (1988) 'Children', in I. Sinclair (ed.), *Residential Care: the research reviewed*, Literature Surveys commissioned by the Independent Preview of Residential Care, London: HMSO.

Payne, C., Douglas, R., and Hansen, P. (1985) *Developing Residential Practice: a source book of references and resources for staff development*, London: National Institute for Social Work.

Pearson, G. (1975) 'The Politics of uncertainty: a study in the socialization of the social worker', in H. Jones (ed.), *Towards a New Social Work*, London: Routledge & Kegan Paul.

Polsky, H. (1965) *Cottage Six*, New York: Wiley.

Polsky, H., Claster, D.S., and Goldberg, C. (eds) (1970) *Social System Perspectives in Residential Institutions*, East Lansing, MI: Michigan State University Press.

Popper, K. (1974) *The Logic of Scientific Discovery*, London: Hutchinson.

Reed, B.D. (1978) *The Dynamics of Religion*, London: Darton, Longman and Todd.

Rice, A.K. (1958) *The Enterprise and its Environment*, London: Tavistock.

Robinson, M. (1984) *Groups*, Chichester: John Wiley and Sons.

Rogers, C.R. (1951) *Client-Centered Therapy*, London: Constable.

Rosenhead, J. (1976) 'Prison "catastrophe"', *New Scientist*, 15 July 1976.

Rousseau, J.-J. (1969) *The Social Contract*, Harmondsworth: Penguin.

Russell, B. (1984) *History of Western Philosophy*, London: Unwin Paperbacks.

Sandler, J., Dare, C., and Holder, A. (1979) *The Patient and the Analyst: the basis of the psychoanalytic process*, London: Maresfield Reprints.

Scott, D. and Starr, I. (1981) 'A 24 hour family-oriented psychiatric and crisis service', *Journal of Family Therapy* 3:177–86.

Seligman, M.E.P. (1974) *Helplessness: depression, development and death*, San Francisco, CA: W.H. Freeman.

Selye, H. (1974) *Stress without Distress*, Philadelphia, DA: Lippincott.

Sinclair, I. (ed.) (1988) *Residential Care: the research reviewed*, Literature Surveys commissioned by the Independent Review of Residential Care, London: HMSO.

Skinner, B.F. (1976) *Walden II*, London: Collier-Macmillan.

Snyder, B.R. (1971) *The Hidden Curriculum*, New York: Alfred A. Knopf.

Steiner, C.M. (1975) *Scripts People Live: transactional analysis of life scripts*, New York: Bantam Books.

Tobin, S. and Lieberman, M.A. (1976) *Last Home for the Aged*, San Francisco, CA: Jossey-Bass.

Townsend, P. (1962) *The Last Refuge: a survey of residential institutions and homes for the aged in England and Wales*, London: Routledge & Kegan Paul.

Tutt, N. (1973) 'Power in residential settings', *Residential Social Work* (June).

Wagner, G. (1988) *A Positive Choice*, Report of the Independent Review of Residential Care, London: HMSO.

Walter, J.A. (1978) *Sent Away: a study of young offenders in care*, Farnborough: Saxon House.

Watzlawick, P., Beavin, D., and Jackson, D. (1967) *The Pragmatics of Human Communication*, New York: W.W. Norton.

Watzlawick, P., Weakland, J., and Fisch, D. (1973) *Change*, New York: Norton.

Weber, M. (1970) *From Max Weber: essays in sociology*, H. Gerth and C. Wright Mills (eds), London: Routledge & Kegan Paul.

Willcocks, D., Peace, S., and Kellaher, L. (1987) *Private Lives in Public Places*, London: Tavistock.

Wills, W.D. (1971) *Spare the Child*, Harmondsworth: Penguin.

Winnicott, D.W. (1980) *Playing and Reality*, Harmondsworth: Penguin.

Wolfensberger, W. (1982) *The Principle of Normalization in Human Services*, Toronto: National Institute of Mental Retardation.

Woodcock, A. and Davis, M. (1980) *Catastrophe Theory*, Harmondsworth: Penguin.

Yablonsky, L. (1967) *Synanon: the tunnel back*, Baltimore, MD: Penguin.

Zimbardo, P.G. (1972) 'Pathology of imprisonment', *Society* (April).

Index